THE
PHENOMENON
OF
LANGUAGE

TABULA LATINA

SECOND EDITION

DAVID J. FLORIAN

Illustrations by
Alex A. Topete

Longman
New York & London

Longman, 10 Bank Street, White Plains, N.Y. 10606

Associated companies:
Longman Group Ltd., London
Longman Cheshire Pty., Melbourne
Longman Paul Pty., Auckland
Copp Clark Pitman, Toronto

Story of Lucius Caecilius Iucundus (p. 20) reprinted by permission from *Cambridge Latin Course, Unit 1,* published by the Syndics of the Cambridge University Press, © Schools Councils Publications, 1970.

Special thanks are due to Ed Phinney for permission to use some of his material from *Cambridge Latin Course, Unit 1, Teacher's Manual* (Cambridge, England: Cambridge University Press, 1983), p. 38 for our Note to the Student (p. 21).

Map on page 226 reprinted by permission from *Ancient Civilization: Rome,* published by Instructo/McGraw-Hill, Paoli, Pennsylvania.

Executive editor: Lyn McLean
Production editor: Marie-Josée A. Schorp
Text design: Jill Francis Wood
Cover design: Thomas Slomka, Thomas William Design
Cover illustration: Alex A. Topete
Text art: Alex A. Topete
Production supervisor: Kathleen M. Ryan

0-8013-0395-8

13141516-HC-03020100999

CONTENTS

PREFACE TO THE TEACHER

The Phenomenon of Language—Tabula Latina is not an introductory Latin course in the traditional sense. That is, it is not simply the first 16 chapters of a typical first-year Latin program, nor does the sequence of materials always follow that of traditional texts. Instead, a great amount of care has been exercised in pre-selecting those concepts which are central to the understanding of Latin grammar but which, at the same time, are transferable to English and to other foreign languages with a minimum of interference from complications or unnecessary exceptions to the rules.

OUR MAIN OBJECTIVES

Our main objectives are 1) to give the student an opportunity to get a "feel" for Latin and how Latin works, 2) to help the student grasp certain basic grammar concepts through the medium of a foreign language, 3) to help the student become aware of the process that language is, 4) to help the student develop generally good language study habits—such as how to go about learning a language, acquiring vocabulary, and so on, and finally 5) to help the student generalize what has been learned about Latin and apply that knowledge to English and other foreign languages.

    The Phenomenon of Language is specifically designed so that *any* teacher, with or without a well-founded background in Latin, can understand the concepts as they are put forth and can teach them. *It does not require an extensive knowledge of Latin to teach the course successfully* and it can easily be individualized.

ANALYSIS EXERCISES—THE ESSENCE OF THE PROGRAM

The essence of the program lies in the *Analysis Exercises*—a series of exercises in which students actively participate in tearing down and rebuilding Latin sentences and structures in an organized way in order to draw conclusions from the process and thereby understand more fully how language is organized. We feel that it is far better in the long run for our students to know HOW to learn rather than simply to accumulate lists of vocabulary items and rules, very few of which are truly clear in their minds. In the *Analysis Exercises*, the process itself is as important as the content.

AN ORIENTATION TOWARD SUCCESS

The Phenomenon of Language is a success-oriented program and includes plenty of positive reinforcement. Drawings and cultural materials that highlight the Roman world have been included in an effort to round out the program. More traditional grammar explanations also find a place in the text when the need arises. A deliberate attempt has been made to provide enough drill exercises of the types found in most foreign language textbooks so that teachers may opt to omit some at their discretion without weakening the effectiveness of the program as a whole.

We firmly believe that a rudimentary knowledge of the *system* behind a language facilitates language learning in general. Students need to progress from being able to carry out a process (which is what happens when language is spoken) to being able to make the process itself the subject of personal perception and, therefore, to bring it under their control. With *The Phenomenon of Language*, we deliberately set out to help our students experience that "process" and learn a "method" of dealing with Language with a capital "L." It encourages them to look, to see, to think, to compare, and finally to draw their own conclusions about language and how language works.

The author wishes to acknowledge most gratefully the considerable time and effort expended by past and present members of the Harvard School Foreign Language Department, North Hollywood, California: Jon Smith, John Corsello, John Graziano, Tim Corcoran, and Roman Brysha. Your contributions through four years of constant evaluation of the developing materials and your constructive criticisms and suggestions have been invaluable in the original production of this work.

Special thanks go also to Marguerite Davis of Independent School Press who carried the banner and waved the flag for lo, these many years. Your support, encouragement, and gentle humor have been very much appreciated and are sorely missed. And to David Greuel, my thanks for your friendship and efforts on behalf of this book. To Rick LaFleur, and much appreciation for undertaking a thorough reading of the present, revised edition. The final product owes a great deal to your recommendations, comments, guidance, and encouragement.

To Lyn McLean and Marie-Josée Schorp at Longman, my eternal gratitude for your endless patience, thoughtful concern, and valiant persistence in seeing me through the maze one more time. And finally, to my wife, Carole, whose patience, support, encouragement, and insights have been invaluable to me both professionally and personally, my love and my thanks.

D. J. F.
Palo Alto, California

PREFACE TO THE STUDENT

BEFORE WE BEGIN, TAKE A MOMENT TO THINK ABOUT THIS

Do you remember the very first day that you came to the school where you are studying now? You were a new person in the school . . . maybe even one of the youngest, too. There were so many things you didn't know. For example, you may not have been sure where you were supposed to go. Where is room 302? Where does that hallway lead? Is history class upstairs or downstairs? What's behind those locked doors? What is it going to be like to study algebra for the first time? Is the cafeteria really on the roof?

There were lots of new faces, too . . . new people whose names you probably didn't know or couldn't remember . . . other students, teachers, administrators, maintenance staff. Everything was new and perhaps a little strange, even mysterious.

But after just a few weeks, you knew perfectly well how to get to room 302, that the hallway which caused you problems on that first day led to the auditorium, and that the cafeteria wasn't really on the roof at all. You already had some idea what algebra was all about and at least you weren't afraid to ask questions when you needed help.

What was happening was that you were learning to depend on and trust your new friends and teachers. What started out being strange, mysterious, new surroundings were becoming more and more familiar to you, and you found that simply because you understood where that hallway led, it quickly lost its quality of mystery.

In short, you were becoming comfortable in your new situation because you UNDERSTOOD how it worked and you were able to use that information to make IT work for YOU. Because you knew the location of the cafeteria, you could get there when you were hungry.

We all find ourselves in new situations like this from time to time throughout our lives. We may change schools, move to a new neighborhood, a new city—even a new country. Later on, you may change jobs, go from being single to being married, and to having a family.

So what does all this have to do with Latin, you may ask

When we begin the study of a foreign language, everything about the other language— its sounds, the way it looks on a written page, the vocabulary, the new grammatical structures, maybe even the alphabet—all of these things make it seem strange and mysterious.

When you go to a new school and can't find room 302 the very first time you try, you don't usually throw up your hands, declare the task impossible and never come back again. No. Instead, you're more apt to give it a second try, this time asking someone for directions. Eventually you succeed in locating the room and when you do, you're well on your way to "de-mystifying" the situation and to bringing it under your control . . . and not letting IT control YOU.

On the other hand, when you approach a whole page of "funny-looking" words in a foreign language text, the temptation is much greater to throw your hands in the air and give up before you even begin. How in the world will you ever make any sense out of all those bizarre words?

Well, if that does happen to you, try to remember how you felt on that first day in your new school. You may not be able to figure it all out on the very first day, or even in the first week, but after just a short time, you will have begun to de-mystify the situation.

Another language or another culture is only
mysterious and strange when we don't understand
how it works and how to make IT work for US.

This book, then, is dedicated to showing you how to go about learning Latin. Once you take the first steps and find that you can succeed, the rest of the journey will be much easier, more rewarding . . . and certainly more fun.

A new challenge . . . Shall we begin?

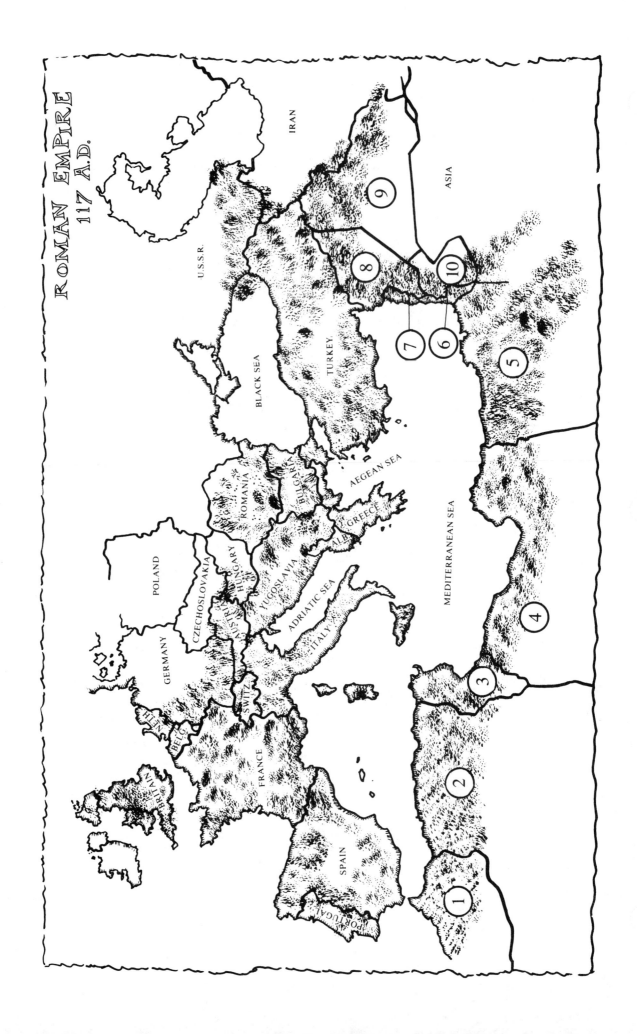

ROMAN EMPIRE
117 A.D.

INTRODUCTION

A Place to Begin

A ROMAN AQUEDUCT

ROME: THE EMPIRE, ITS LANGUAGE, AND ITS PEOPLE

The Latin language has often been described as a so-called "dead" language because it is no longer the official language of any country in the modern world. The civilization that spoke Latin faded away after the collapse of the Roman Empire in 476 A.D. The Latin spoken in each of the different Roman provinces was eventually replaced by other "modern" languages like French, Spanish, Italian, Romanian, and Portuguese.

Yet even if the Roman Empire no longer exists today and Latin is no longer the spoken language of any country in the world, the ideas and the language of ancient Rome have probably had more influence on our daily lives than any other culture that ever existed. Did you know, for example, that even something as personal and local as the graduation exercises at your own school have probably been directly influenced by Rome?

"Now, how can that be?" you may ask. "What in the world do graduation exercises have to do with the Romans?" If you read on, there's a good chance that you'll find out.

ROME AND THE EMPIRE

The Roman Empire was at its peak of glory in 117 A.D. The borders of Rome extended to the continents of Europe, Asia, and Africa and encircled the entire Mediterranean Sea (see map opposite page I). The city of Rome itself was the hub of the Empire and the center of the government. It was a sophisticated and cultured city. As the powerful Roman legions moved farther and farther from Rome to conquer new and distant lands, they took with them the Roman language, laws, and culture, which were quickly absorbed and adopted by the conquered peoples. By 117 A.D., all of the present-day countries that surround the Mediterranean Sea were united under the umbrella of Rome—speaking one language, having one code of laws, and sharing in the brilliance and splendor of the Empire.

The Romans were master builders and architects. Everywhere they went, they joined the far-flung reaches of the Empire together by building magnificent roads, sturdy bridges, aqueducts, temples, and public baths and amphitheaters for sport and entertainment. They were such good builders, in fact, that parts of the Appian Way, the "superhighway" of the ancient world, are still in use even today, 2,000 years later!

And the Appian Way is not the only Roman relic still in existence. Many other Roman structures are still standing, also. Some continue to be used, some have become popular tourist attractions, and others simply lie in ruins, dotting the countryside and sharing the fields with grazing cattle and passing motorists.

ROME, LATIN, AND THE IMPORTANCE OF LANGUAGE

With all of these roads, bridges, temples, and other structures, the Romans left us many tangible reminders of their once powerful presence. But probably one of the greatest contributions that the Romans left behind is their language. That may seem like a strange statement to make, but it's true.

Language is a funny thing. Usually, it's just sort of "there." Of course, we use it all the time, so we take it pretty much for granted. In fact, we don't usually think much about the language we speak until we have to take a grammar exam or study language in school.

But the language we use to express our thoughts, our needs, our likes and dislikes is a very personal and very powerful thing. Whole nations have gone to war over language. Thousands upon thousands of people have died because one group has tried to impose its language on another group that spoke a different language. To be deprived of our means of communication with the world is a very serious and very threatening situation.

Imagine how you would feel if the principal of your school suddenly decided that from this day forward, you would not be allowed to conduct any school business in English, but would have to use some other language instead. All your classes—math, physical education, social studies, science, everything—would have to be taught in this new language, and all the discussion in class would have to be conducted in this language, also. Of course, you wouldn't be able to speak English during lunch or recess, either. How do you think you would react to such a situation? Do you think it would be easy? Fun? Frustrating? Difficult? How would it change your life?

Now imagine that there was a club or organization in your school that you admired greatly and wanted very much to join. The activities they planned were always more fun and more enjoyable than any other organization around. But to belong to the club and enjoy the benefits of membership you would have to learn the special rules that governed the group, including the special language they used to conduct their meetings. If you *really* wanted to participate in their activities, how do you think that would affect your attitude about learning their new language? How would it differ from the example outlined in the last paragraph?

Well, it was a little like that wherever the Roman legions went. Naturally, the language they spoke was Latin. All official government business was conducted in the Latin language, and they expected the people they conquered to learn and to speak Latin, too. But because Rome was such a progressive civilization for its time and most of the cultures the Romans conquered were much weaker and less developed, the conquered peoples were usually quite eager to adopt the language of the more sophisticated Romans because it meant that they could enjoy the greater benefits of a more advanced society.

When a strong culture meets a weaker culture, the weak culture often loses its language.

THE END OF THE EMPIRE AND ITS EFFECT ON LATIN

There were many reasons why the Roman Empire began to weaken and fall apart. We will leave that study to another time. But as the power of Rome diminished and became less of a uniting world force, each area of the Empire grew more independent of the central government and less dependent on Rome for all its needs.

Even though Latin continued to be the official language, we must remember that each distinct area of the Empire spoke its own provincial dialect of Latin. For example, English is the official language of the United States, but southerners, New Englanders, midwesterners, and westerners (not to mention the British, the Australians, etc.) speak it with different "accents" and have their own regionalisms and expressions that make each English "dialect" colorful and interesting in its own way.

With the weakening of Rome's influence over its many provinces, there was no longer a strong central government to set the standard for the language. Each separate area began to develop its own brand of Latin. There were the French who spoke it with a "French" accent, the Spanish who spoke it with a "Spanish" accent, and so forth. The Latin of each region began to develop in a different way from the Latin of the other regions until, finally, each province was speaking "Latin" so differently that one group could no longer understand the "Latin" of the others.

Remember, even with the good Roman roads, travel was difficult and often hazardous in Roman times. People from one area were not in constant contact with people from other areas as they are today with our modern jets, televisions, computers, and satellites to help speed communication and travel.

Today, French, Italian, Portuguese, Romanian, and Spanish are known as the "Romance" languages because they developed directly from the Latin of the Romans. You'll notice that our own English, a member of the Germanic family of languages, is not listed among them. Yet we will discover later in this book that approximately 65 percent of all English words come to us from Latin, anyway.

LATIN	MATER	AQUA
ITALIAN	Madre	Acqua
Spanish	Madre	Agua
Portuguese	Mãe	Água
ROMANIAN	MAMĂ	APĂ
French	Mère	Eau

THE INFLUENCE OF ROME AFTER THE FALL OF THE EMPIRE

Just because Rome no longer maintained a stronghold on what was once a vast empire, the impact of Rome did not stop when the Empire did. Not at all. In fact, the influence of the ancient Romans continued to spread to other, even more remote parts of the world. Adventurous Europeans, who no longer called themselves Romans but thought of themselves as Spaniards, Italians, Portuguese, or French men and women, continued to seek new and exotic lands to conquer. Yet these people were the direct descendants of the Romans and their subjects who lived under the Empire in earlier times.

And if all of the great Roman structures did not survive the journey through time completely intact, many public buildings in major (and some not so major) cities throughout the world have copied the Roman models. In our own Washington, D.C., for example, many of the government buildings—including the U.S. Capitol building—were designed to resemble ancient Roman temples. The very word "capitol" comes to us from the Latin word *capitolium*, which was the ancient temple to Jupiter located on the Capitoline hill in Rome, the center of Roman religion.

And Roman architecture is certainly not the only Roman influence we see about us in the modern world. The very foundations of our representative form of government have their roots in the Roman code of laws. In fact, to this day, many law schools still require their students to take a course in Roman law, and we continue to elect *senators* to represent us in the *Senate* of the U.S. Congress much as the Romans did in the Senate of Rome.

It's no wonder, then, that even today we study Latin and the society that spoke that language. The influence of Rome was so great that even 2,000 years later, we still see it about us in our lives every day. We see it in our architecture and in the laws that govern our behavior (and our rights!). We see it in thousands of scientific and technical terms—most of them borrowed directly from Latin—that have been adopted or created to keep up with new technological advances. In fact, Latin appears in countless other words that we use every day from virtually every field of endeavor. And, yes, we see the influence of Rome even in the judicial robes of our judges and in the gowns we wear at our graduation ceremonies to celebrate the completion of our studies. Those gowns are modeled after . . . you guessed it . . . the Roman toga (see page CXXXVI).

To study the life, language, and customs of the early Romans, then, is to study our own roots and to understand better our own modern civilization. In addition, studying the Latin language has important side effects on our ability to understand our own English vocabulary and grammar. It helps us improve our ability to spell in English and to increase our understanding of more and more English words. In fact, studying Latin will even help us to learn and to understand other foreign languages.

These, then, are precisely the goals that we can expect to accomplish by completing this book. It has been especially designed to take every advantage that Latin offers us to make our understanding of our own language easier, more fun and more profitable, and to pave the way for the further study of Latin and of other languages and cultures as well.

Now that the first pages have been read and the introductions made, *Iacta alea est* ("the die is cast"), to quote a famous Roman soldier. Shall we begin?

Many scientific terms come directly from Latin.

＿＿＿＿＿＿＿＿＿＿＿＿＿＿ **I. QUAESTIŌNĒS** ＿＿＿＿＿＿＿＿＿＿＿＿＿

A) ROME AND THE ROMANS. Circle the response that best completes each sentence. Please circle *the entire answer* and not just the letter that precedes it.

1. The people of Rome spoke
    a) Roman **b)** Italian **c)** Latin **d)** Romanche

2. The Roman Empire was at its peak in
    a) the second century A.D. **b)** the fourteenth century A.D.
    c) the eighth century B.C.

3. The Roman Empire included
    a) all of Europe and Africa **b)** the Mediterranean world
    c) all of Asia

4. Latin became the common language of a good part of what is now known as Europe, North Africa, and the Middle East because
    a) Rome was very powerful, and when a strong culture meets a weaker culture, the weaker culture often loses its language.
    b) Latin could be used more effectively to deal with the day-to-day living situations of the common people in all parts of the Empire.
    c) Latin was easier to learn than Celtic.

5. The Appian Way is a famous Roman
    a) political philosophy **b)** law **c)** road

6. The "Romance" languages are so named because
    a) they are spoken in "exotic," romantic lands.
    b) they are rich in words that express love.
    c) they are based largely on the language of the Romans.

7. Below is a list of eight languages. Indicate those five that are known as "Romance" languages.

    a) Portuguese   **e)** Romanian
    b) Spanish   **f)** Greek
    c) Bulgarian   **g)** French
    d) Italian   **h)** Hungarian

8. English is NOT considered one of the Romance languages. We will learn why

later. Nevertheless, _____ percent of all English words are derived directly or
indirectly from Latin.
a) approximately 50 percent   b) approximately 25 percent
c) probably less than 40 percent d) approximately 65 percent

9. The Romance languages developed as separate languages because
a) as the Roman Empire weakened and the power of Rome declined, the Latin
spoken in each area of the Empire developed in a different way due to a lack
of constant communication.
b) the people in the areas that Rome dominated did not want to continue speaking Latin, the language of their conquerors.
c) after the fall of the Roman Empire, each province decided what language it
wanted to adopt as the official language of that region.

10. The study of Latin can help us (circle all answers that are correct)
a) to understand English grammar better.
b) to improve our English vocabulary and spelling.
c) to learn and to understand other foreign languages more easily.
d) to appreciate the basis of our representative form of government.

B) Look at the map of the Roman Empire facing page I. At the height of its power,
Rome's influence extended over the entire shaded area that touched three continents:
Europe, Africa, and Asia. Superimposed on the shaded area, you will see the boundaries
of the many present-day nations into which the Roman Empire was eventually divided.
Only the European nations are labeled. The names of the African and Asian nations
are missing.
    Consult a world atlas to fill in the names of the present-day African and Asian
countries that were once a part of the Roman Empire. Write each answer next to the
corresponding number.

1. _____   6. _____

2. _____   7. _____

3. _____   8. _____

4. _____   9. _____

5. _____   10. _____

A Few Words about Classical Latin Pronunciation: Why Learn How to Pronounce It If It Is No Longer a Spoken Language?

Latin and the Catholic Church

The only place in the world where Latin is actually spoken today is in the Roman Catholic Church. Of course, in order to keep the language current with modern developments, the Church must constantly update Latin vocabulary and create the new words needed to discuss new technological and social developments that did not exist at the time of the Roman Empire (and for which there are, of course, no classical Latin words). For instance, how would we say *helicopter, light bulb,* or *computer* in Latin?

Because the seat of the Roman Catholic Church is in the Vatican (actually an independent papal state) in Rome, it is not surprising to learn that the Latin used by the modern Church is pronounced as if it were Italian. This pronunciation is quite different from the way the Romans of Julius Caesar's time pronounced their language.

How do we know that? Of course, we don't have any recordings or videotapes of Cicero's speeches before the Senate to help us determine just what those differences are. And even though Julius Caesar was a powerful politician, he never appeared before the citizens of Rome on television. Yet, by studying and comparing old Roman texts, linguists have been able to reconstruct to a great degree how the ancient Romans pronounced their language.

Classical Latin

In this book, we will learn (and use) the classical Latin pronunciation of ancient Rome. Fortunately for us, Latin is a highly *phonetic* language. That means that it is pronounced exactly the way it is spelled. Is that true of English? How would you explain to a foreigner, for example, why words like *pneumonia, knife, through,* and *bright* are spelled the way they are with all of those extra letters that are not pronounced? Or consider an outsider's confusion upon first meeting the English word *yacht.* There is no way on earth that he or she could guess, without being told, that the *ch* is silent in that word!

But Latin pronunciation is very regular—much simpler than English. First of all, there are no silent letters in Latin. Every letter that is written is pronounced. Each consonant has only one sound, and vowels can be pronounced in one of only two different ways. With a few easy rules, then, we can learn to pronounce Latin as its original Roman speakers did. This will be especially helpful if we ever decide to study any of the modern Romance languages. Many of the rules that apply to classical Latin pronunciation apply to them as well, so we will already have a lot of information about how other foreign languages are pronounced.

The best way to learn the sounds of a language, of course, is to repeat and to imitate them directly. Using the few basic rules that we have listed below as a guide, you will be able to imitate the sounds of Latin accurately.

CICERO: IS IT PRONOUNCED "SISSY-RO" OR "KICK-ER-RO"?

THE ALPHABET

Because our own alphabet is based on the letters handed down to us by the Romans, it is not surprising to find that the form of the letters of the Latin alphabet is identical to the form of our English letters. But the roots of our alphabet go back even further than that, all the way back, in fact, to the Greeks and their alphabet.

Greece was a sophisticated and powerful nation when the Romans were still a relatively primitive tribe on the banks of the Tiber River. Greek sea merchants traded with the Etruscans, another people who lived on the west coast of Italy and who were neighbors of the early Romans. In order to do business with the Greek traders, the Etruscans learned to write the Greek language and finally adapted the Greek alphabet to their own language, changing the letters here and there to suit their particular needs. The Romans, in turn, borrowed the writing system of the Etruscans and used it to write Latin.

The earliest inscriptions that have been found written in the Latin language (700 to 500 B.C.) used only 21 letters. As Rome grew in power and influence, the Romans expanded beyond their own borders, absorbing the cultures of the nations they conquered, which eventually included Greece itself!

The Romans particularly admired the Greeks and were greatly influenced by them and their civilization. By the end of the first century B.C., so many new words and ideas had been borrowed from the Greeks that the Romans added the Greek letters Y and Z to the end of their own alphabet to accommodate the new sounds needed to pronounce these new words. In later times, the letters J, U, and W were also added as variants of the Roman letters I and V. The letter K, although part of the Latin alphabet, was eventually replaced in many words by C.

VOWELS: AOEIU

Latin Vowels and Their Approximate English Equivalents

Each vowel in Latin has two sounds—a long sound and a short one. For the vowels A and O, the difference between long and short is a difference of *quantity*, that is, the difference lies in the *length of time* the vowel is pronounced. There is no change in the sound itself.

LONG	SHORT
a as in father	a as in idea
o as in nose	o as in omit

For the vowels *E, I, U*, the difference between long and short is a difference of *quality*. That is, there is actually a change in the sound of the vowel. Look at the following examples:

LONG	SHORT
ē as in café	e as in bed
ī as in machine	i as in tin
ū as in rude (never as in pupil)	u as in put

To help you pronounce Latin more accurately, all long vowels in this book are marked with a **macron** (ā, ō, ē, ī, ū); short vowels remain unmarked. The Romans themselves did not use macrons in their writing. Invented by more modern scholars, **macrons** serve as helpful reminders to us as we learn to read and to pronounce a new language.

DIPHTHONGS

Diphthongs are combinations of two vowels that make a single sound. Observe:

ae is pronounced like the ai in aisle
au is pronounced like the ow in now
ei is pronounced like the ei in neighbor
eu is pronounced like e + u (short)
oe is pronounced like the oi in oil
ui is pronounced like the uee in queen

Doubled vowels are not diphthongs and are pronounced separately:

suus is pronounced "su-us"

CONSONANTS

Although most consonants in Latin are pronounced essentially as they are in standard English, there are a few exceptions. They are listed below.

c is pronounced as in cat (never soft, as in city)
g is pronounced as in game (never soft, as in gem)
s is pronounced as in same (never as in rose)
t is pronounced as in tea (never "sh" as in nation)
v is pronounced as the w in win (never as in vampire)
x is pronounced "ks" as in extra (never "gz" as in exam)
ch is pronounced like k
ph is pronounced like p
th is pronounced like t

The Vowel "I" Used as a Consonant

When the letter *I* is the first letter of a word and is immediately followed by a vowel (*Iulius, iustus*), it is pronounced as the *Y* in *yes*.

In this instance, the *I* is no longer considered a vowel, but a consonant. In the later years of the Empire, the consonant *I* was often replaced by a newer addition to the Latin alphabet, the letter *J*. You will probably recognize our two examples above as the name *Julius* and the English word *just* (as in justice).

A Few Things to Remember about Stress and Accent

1. Never stress the last syllable of a word.
2. In two-syllable words, stress the first syllable. (*Rō'ma*)
3. In words of more than two syllables,
   a) stress the *next-to-last* syllable when
      the next-to-last syllable is long (*ma-gis-trā'-tus*)
      there are any two consonants (except L and R) immediately after the vowel (*con-ti-nen'-tes*)
   b) stress the *third-to-last* syllable
      in all other cases (*a-gri'-co-la*)

MARCUS TULLIUS CICERO 106 BC.– 43 BC.

LECTIO I

What's in a Name?

SALLUSTIUS   MANDŪCUS   SEMPRŌNIA   POPPAEA

Every culture has its own way to name the individuals that make up that culture. In the section that follows, you will find two lists of Roman names, one for men and one for women. These lists are by no means complete. Not all of the names were used as first names by the Romans, and those with asterisks were borrowed from the Greeks. Many of them, however, are still common today in English or in other languages, often in a slightly changed form. Do you recognize some of them?

See how well you can pronounce the names on these lists using the pronunciation guide in the introduction.

MEN'S NAMES

Actius	Fābricius	Maximus	Silvānus
Aemilius	Gāius	Octāvius	Stronnius
Antōnius	Grumio*	Paulus	Tacitus
Atticus	Horātius	Pompōnius	Tēlemachus*
Caecilius	Iūlius	Publius	Terentius
Caedicius	Līvineius	Pugnax	Tiberius
Casellius	Līvius	Quintus	Tīro
Celer	Lūcius	Rēgulus	Titus
Claudius	Lūcrētius	Rufus	Trānio*
Clēmens	Lūcrīo	Sallustius	Trebius
Cornēlius	Mandūcus	Scīpio	Tullius*
Davus	Marcellus	Secundus	Vergilius
Decimus	Marcus	Sextus	
Decius	Marius	Sīlēnus	

WOMEN'S NAMES

Aemilia	Drūsīlla	Maria	Silvia
Alma	Flāvia	Matella	Stella
Anna	Gāia	Melissa	Terentia
Antōnia	Horātia	Octāvia	Tullia
Arria	Hortensia	Paula	Valeria
Aurelia	Iūlia	Paulīna	Virginia
Caecilia	Lāvīnia	Poppaea	Zōē*
Calpurnia	Līvia	Portia	
Camilla	Lūcīlia	Quintia	
Clāra	Lūcrētia	Scribōnia	
Claudia	Marcella	Secunda	
Cornēlia	Marcia	Semprōnia	

MR. AND MRS.

_____ I. EXERCITĀTIŌ _____

Use the list of Roman names below to practice your Latin pronunciation. Decide which of the English choices given contains *the same* or *nearly the same* sound as the underlined portion of the Latin word. Indicate your answer by placing an X in the space provided.

1. Vir<u>g</u>inia

_____ <u>g</u>entle

_____ <u>g</u>ive

_____ mer<u>g</u>e

_____ bri<u>g</u>ht

2. Tēlema<u>ch</u>us

_____ mu<u>ch</u>

_____ <u>c</u>alendar

_____ pla<u>c</u>e

_____ <u>sh</u>ow

3. P<u>au</u>lus

_____ B<u>o</u>ston

_____ <u>o</u>ver

_____ b<u>ow</u>ling

_____ p<u>ow</u>der

4. Mar<u>c</u>ella

_____ <u>c</u>itizen

_____ mar<u>sh</u>mallow

_____ mar<u>k</u>et

_____ sin<u>g</u>le

5. C<u>ae</u>dicius

_____ s<u>a</u>ve

_____ s<u>a</u>lamander

_____ <u>i</u>dol

_____ <u>i</u>nterest

6. Horā<u>ti</u>us

_____ <u>t</u>eenager

_____ ra<u>ti</u>on

_____ me<u>ss</u>

_____ se<u>ts</u>

7. Flā<u>v</u>ia

_____ e<u>v</u>en

_____ <u>w</u>itness

_____ a<u>ff</u>ect

_____ reser<u>v</u>oir

8. <u>O</u>ctāvia

_____ z<u>oo</u>

_____ b<u>o</u>ther

_____ br<u>o</u>ther

_____ <u>o</u>rnament

9. Marc<u>u</u>s

_____ f<u>u</u>ss

_____ g<u>oo</u>se

_____ f<u>ew</u>

_____ m<u>u</u>te

10. Mandū<u>c</u>us

_____ f<u>u</u>ss

_____ g<u>oo</u>se

_____ f<u>ew</u>

_____ m<u>u</u>te

11. Atti<u>c</u>us

_____ p<u>i</u>ne

_____ ca<u>si</u>no

_____ po<u>ssi</u>ble

_____ accl<u>ai</u>m

12. Paul<u>ī</u>na

_____ p<u>i</u>ne

_____ ca<u>si</u>no

_____ po<u>ssi</u>ble

_____ accl<u>ai</u>m

_____ **II. ANALYSIS EXERCISE** _____

GENDER AND LATIN ENDINGS

> ## ANALYSIS QUESTION
>
> **Do most Roman proper names follow a pattern?**

Refer to the list of Roman names on page XIII to answer the following questions.

1. There are 54 men's names listed. With the exception of just eight, all the other names on the list end with these last two letters:

    _____

2. In the spaces below, write the names from the men's list that *do not* end in these two letters. Write them in alphabetical order and be sure to include the macron when needed.

    a) _____   e) _____

    b) _____   f) _____

    c) _____   g) _____

    d) _____   h) _____

3. There are 43 women's names listed. With the exception of just one, all the others end with the letter:

    _____

    (The exception? Write the whole name on the line below.)

    _____

NÕMEN _____

DIĒS _____

Now look back at the information we collected in the three questions above and complete the following sentences by writing the correct answer from those given.

4. Roman names that end in **-us** are probably names of _____.
    (MEN/WOMEN)

5. Roman names that end in **-a** are probably names of _____.
    (MEN/WOMEN)

6. **-us** and **-a** seem to be the most common endings for Latin names.

    _____
    (TRUE/FALSE)

7. Other endings on names _____ occur.
    (NEVER/SOMETIMES/ALWAYS)

Taking into consideration all of the observations you've made so far about Roman proper names, now you're ready to draw your own conclusion about the Analysis Question asked at the beginning of the exercise. Fill in the blanks below with the appropriate responses:

CONCLUSION

1. Most Roman men had names that ended in _____.

2. Most Roman women had names that ended in _____.

3. Roman names _____ had other endings.
    (ALWAYS/SOMETIMES/NEVER)

4. ANALYSIS ANSWER: Therefore, there _____ a general
    (WAS/WAS NOT)
    pattern to most Roman names.

DID YOU KNOW . . . ?

Latin is no longer spoken in any country of the world today, but did you know that as late as 1848, Latin was the official language of both Hungary and Croatia? (Croatia is now a part of Yugoslavia.)

In addition, one could still hear conversations in Latin between students and teachers on the streets of the "Latin Quarter" in Paris (France) until the end of the 19th century. The "Latin Quarter" got its name from the fact that Latin originally was the official language of the Sorbonne, the first college of the University of Paris, founded in 1253 A.D. Because students from many different countries attended classes there and because the Sorbonne was originally a school for theological studies, all classes were taught in Latin.

_____ III. EXERCITĀTIŌNĒS _____

A) Looking at the two lists of Roman names at the beginning of Chapter I, you will notice that some of the names appear both on the list of men's names and on the list of women's names, each, of course, carrying the proper endings. Here are 10 such names from the lists. We have given you the masculine forms. Write their feminine counterparts in the blanks provided. Be careful to include the macrons when necessary. Can you find more pairs on the lists?

	MASCULINE	FEMININE		MASCULINE	FEMININE
1.	Aemilius	_____	6.	Līvius	_____
2.	Caecilius	_____	7.	Lūcrētius	_____
3.	Gāius	_____	8.	Marcellus	_____
4.	Claudius	_____	9.	Octāvius	_____
5.	Iūlius	_____	10.	Paulus	_____

B) Do English names have both a masculine and feminine form sometimes? Take a look at the list of women's names below and write the proper masculine form in the blanks on the right.

	FEMININE	MASCULINE		FEMININE	MASCULINE
1.	Henrietta	_____	5.	Julia	_____
2.	Roberta	_____	6.	Paula	_____
3.	Pauline	_____	7.	Georgina	_____
4.	Cecilia	_____	8.	Alberta	_____

C) Here are some new Latin names.

1. What is the feminine equivalent of

    Fābulus _____

    Iūnius _____

    Albius _____

2. What is the masculine equivalent of

    Porcia _____

    Ovidia _____

    Persia _____

    Catulla _____

D) Many Roman names have survived to the present day and are commonly in use in the English-speaking world. Sometimes their spelling has changed slightly on their journey through the centuries. Can you match the following English names to their ancient Roman counterparts? Be careful of the proper gender (masculine or feminine) and be sure to include the macrons where needed.

ENGLISH NAME	LATIN ANCESTOR		ENGLISH NAME	LATIN ANCESTOR
1. Paul	_____	6.	Julius	_____
2. Mark	_____	7.	Emily	_____
3. Tony (Anthony)	_____	8.	Cecilia	_____
4. Sylvia	_____	9.	Cecil	_____
5. Virginia	_____	10.	Terry (Terrence)	_____

E) Try matching these typical French, Italian, Romanian, and Spanish names to their Latin ancestors. Note the indications (m.) and (f.) for masculine and feminine.

	MODERN NAME	COUNTRY	LATIN ANCESTOR
1.	Marcel (m.)	France	_____
2.	Camille (f.)	France	_____
3.	Virgil (m.)	Romania	_____
4.	Liviu (m.)	Romania	_____
5.	Aurelia (f.)	Romania	_____
6.	Máximo (m.)	Spain	_____
7.	María (f.)	Spain	_____
8.	Mario (m.)	Italy	_____
9.	Fabrizio (m.)	Italy	_____
10.	Silvana (f.)	Italy	_____

LECTIO II

Meeting the Romans

Caecilius lived in Pompeii at the foot of Mount Vesuvius.

NARRĀTIO

LŪCIUS CAECILIUS IŪCŬNDUS

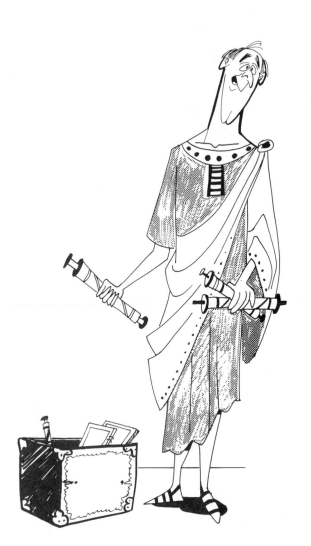

Caecilius lived in Italy during the first century A.D. in the town of Pompeii. This town had a population of about 20,000 and was situated at the foot of Mount Vesuvius on the coast of the Bay of Naples. Caecilius was a wealthy Pompeian banker. His business records, which were discovered when his house was excavated, tell us that he was also an auctioneer, tax collector, farmer, and moneylender.

Some of his wealth he inherited from his father, Lūcius Caecilius Fēlix, but he probably acquired most of it through his own shrewd and energetic business activities. He dealt in slaves, cloth, timber, and property. He also carried on a cleaning and dyeing business, grazed herds of sheep or cattle on pastureland outside the town, and he sometimes won the contract for collecting the local taxes. He may have owned a few shops as well. As a moneylender, he probably helped local shipping companies to finance their overseas trade. The profits on such deals were often very large.

We can also discover more about Caecilius by looking carefully at his full name, which was Lūcius Caecilius Iūcundus. Only a full Roman citizen would have three names. A slave would have only one name. As a Roman citizen, Caecilius not only had the right to vote in elections, but also was fully protected by the law against injustice and loss of freedom. The many slaves who lived and worked in his house and his businesses had no rights of their own. They were his property and he could treat them well or badly as he wished. There was one important exception to this rule. The law did not permit a master to execute a slave without showing good reason.

Caecilius's first name was Lūcius. This was rather like our given name. His second name was Caecilius and this shows that he was a member of the "clan" of the Caecilii. Clans or family groups were very important, and strong feelings of loyalty existed within them. Caecilius's third name, Iūcundus, indicates his own immediate family. The word *iūcundus* means *pleasant*, just as in English we find surnames like *Merry* or *Jolly*.

Lūcius Caecilius Iūcundus was a real person. His address in Pompeii was Regio V, Insula I, number 26. Caecilius's house has been excavated from the ruins of the city and can be visited today by tourists. Number 26 is indicated on the archaeological grid maps of the city of Pompeii, and until recently was famous for a marble relief in one of its rooms that depicted the forum being shaken in the earthquake of 63 A.D. Unfortunately, the relief was stolen a number of years ago and has never been recovered.

Caecilius had detailed records of his business dealings, which he kept on 153 waxed tablets stored in a strongbox in his house. The tablets were discovered in 1875 by archaeologists digging in the vicinity. The National Museum in Naples houses artifacts excavated in Pompeii along with a bronze bust that was also found in the house. The bust of a middle-aged man with a wart on his chin was probably the portrait of Caecilius's father or some other close relative.

Translations of some of Caecilius's business records have been published in *Roman Civilization: A Sourcebook: II: The Empire* by Lewis and Reinhold (New York: Harper & Row, 1966).

GLASS CLINKING

Gladiators drank a glass of wine before entering the arena to duel. However, in order to insure that neither had poisoned or drugged the other's drink, they customarily touched glasses and mixed the wine from both glasses before downing what was usually, for one of them at least, a *last* drink. We still continue this custom of clinking glasses today when toasting with friends at social gatherings.

_____ **I. QUAESTIŌNĒS** _____

LŪCIUS CAECILIUS IŪCUNDUS. Complete the following sentences with the word or words needed. Be careful that your spelling is correct.

1. Caecilius was a real person who lived in the town of _____ .

His principal occupation was _____ .

2. Caecilius's full name was

_____ .

3. We know that he was a full Roman citizen because

_____ .

4. If a man in Rome were known only as Trānio and had no other names, we would guess that he was probably a _____ .

5. The name Caecilius shows that our Roman was a member of the _____ of the Caecilii.

NŌMEN _____

DIĒS _____

II. EXPLICĀTIŌNĒS

WRITING NUMBERS THE ROMAN WAY

We are all familiar with Roman numerals because we find them in many places. They appear frequently on clocks, in chapter headings in books, and in outlines. We even find them in the movies! In fact, the next time you go to a movie, watch the credits at the end of the film. The year in which it was made is usually indicated in Roman numerals. *Gone With The Wind*, for example, was filmed in MCMXXXIX.

Roman numerals are a good example of just how consistently our everyday lives are still touched by a great civilization that existed in the distant past. Of course, they are called "Roman" because this is the numbering system that was used by the ancient Romans. Compared to our modern "Arabic" numbers (1, 2, 3, etc.), Roman numerals can be clumsy and difficult to work with. Still, it was better than no numbering system at all, and it worked very nicely for the needs of the Romans.

_____	I	ūnus, ūna, ūnum	_____	XVII	septendecim
_____	II	duo, duae, duo	_____	XVIII	duodēvīgintī
_____	III	trēs, tria	_____	XIX	ūndēvīgintī
_____	IV	quattuor	_____	XX	vīgintī
_____	V	quīnque	_____	XXX	trīgintā
_____	VI	sex	_____	XL	quadrāgintā
_____	VII	septem	_____	L	quīnquāgintā
_____	VIII	octō	_____	LX	sexāgintā
_____	IX	novem	_____	LXX	septuāgintā
_____	X	decem	_____	LXXX	octōgintā
_____	XI	ūndecim	_____	XC	nōnāgintā
_____	XII	duodecim	_____	C	centum
_____	XIII	trēdecim	_____	CC	ducentī
_____	XIV	quattuordecim	_____	D	quīngentī
_____	XV	quindecim	_____	M	mīlle
_____	XVI	sēdecim			

The Roman system of numbering was based on the very simple principle of counting on the fingers. Among the Greeks and Romans, finger counting was a highly developed and elaborate skill that was carefully taught in the schools. Certain fingers of each hand were designated to represent units, tens, hundreds, and thousands. By bending the fingers at different angles and by placing the hands on different parts of the body, complicated mathematical calculations could be performed and communicated to others solely by using finger signs.

In order to write their numbers down, the Romans began by copying the simplest finger indications. One finger held up (*I*) meant, of course, the number *one*. Two raised fingers (*II*) indicated *two*, and three vertical fingers (*III*) meant *three*. It was simple to represent these with one, two, or three single strokes of a pen. The number *five* was represented by a V to mimic the space between the thumb and all four fingers held close together.

Of course, this system of representing numbers with fingers can only work as long as you have enough fingers. It would not be very practical, for instance, to show one hundred fingers to represent the number *100*. To make their written numbering system more convenient, the Romans settled on a system of addition and subtraction to represent larger numbers—depending on the placement of certain letters. Putting one or two or three lines *after* a V, for example, would mean that you wanted to *add* one or two or three to the number five. Look at the examples below:

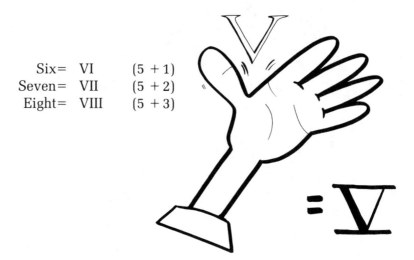

Six=	VI	(5 + 1)
Seven=	VII	(5 + 2)
Eight=	VIII	(5 + 3)

The Romans limited the number of vertical lines *after* another number to *three*. However, inserting a vertical line *before* V meant that you wished to *decrease* that number by one: IV = (5 − 1) or *four*. They limited the number of vertical lines *before* another number to *one*.

The number "ten" was represented by two Vs placed tip to tip to form an X. Using the standard addition/subtraction rule, we can write the following numbers:

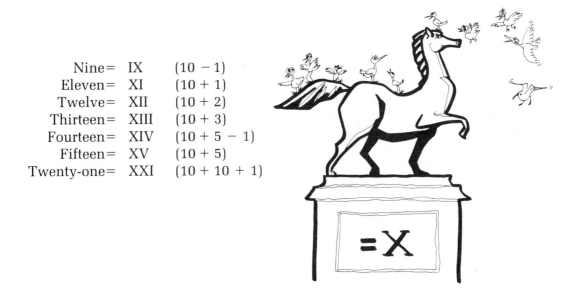

Nine=	IX	(10 − 1)
Eleven=	XI	(10 + 1)
Twelve=	XII	(10 + 2)
Thirteen=	XIII	(10 + 3)
Fourteen=	XIV	(10 + 5 − 1)
Fifteen=	XV	(10 + 5)
Twenty-one=	XXI	(10 + 10 + 1)

Getting Fancy

When you think about it, this simple system is quite ingenious. It enabled the Romans to write all of the numbers from 1 to 40. To write larger numbers, the Romans added other letters. From Greek (by way of the Etruscans), they took the letter *L* to represent "50". The number "40" can be written two different ways:

Forty	= XXXX	(10 + 10 + 10 + 10)	
	XL	(50 − 10)	
Sixty	= LX	(50 + 10)	
Seventy	= LXX	(50 + 10 + 10)	Et cetera . . .

The number *100* is represented by the letter *C*, the first letter of the word *centum*, which means *one hundred* in Latin. In the same manner, they used *M* to stand for *1,000* from the Latin word for one thousand, *mīlle*. *Five hundred* was represented by the letter *D*, probably for *demi-mīlle* or *one-half of one thousand*.

By using just these few letters to represent numbers plus an organized system to indicate addition and subtraction, the Romans were able to write more complicated numbers simply by putting the letters next to each other.

MCDXLII = 1000 + (500 − 100) + (50 − 10) + 2 = 1,442

$$\text{M} \qquad \text{CD} \qquad \text{XL} \quad \text{II}$$

NŌMEN _____

DIĒS _____

The Arabs Had a Better Way

The Arabs developed a far superior and more sophisticated numbering system which they based on ideas they borrowed from India. To the Indian numbering system, the Arabs added the concepts of *zero* and *place value*. This enabled them to use the same numbers *one* through *nine* over and over again by assigning different values to them simply by adding zeroes. For example, the numbers *9, 90, 900,* and *9,000* are vastly different numbers, yet they use only *two* different numerals: *9* and *0.*

The invention of zero allowed the Arabs to simplify their system of calculating and to do still more complicated kinds of calculations. Yet it wasn't until the 12th century A.D. that Europe abandoned the less convenient Roman system in favor of the Arabic system.

Today, Arabic numerals are used in all international trade and almost universally in scientific work. In fact, it is the Arabic system of numbering that is used in most parts of the world even though the actual shape of the numbers themselves has changed substantially over the centuries. The invention of the printing press in the 15th century helped to standardize those shapes into the familiar numbers we recognize today.

Although Roman numerals still have a place in our modern world, we would be in big trouble with our calculators and computers if we *only* had Roman numerals with which to work. Do the simple arithmetic problem below by filling in the blanks with the Arabic equivalents of all of the Roman numerals, then translate your answer into Roman numerals as well. Do you think you would like to have your entire math book written in Roman numerals?

MCCXXXIX + DCCXLVIII − CCXCIII ÷ II = _____

_____ + _____ − _____ ÷ __ = _____

NŌMEN _____

DIĒS _____

_____ III. EXERCITĀTIŌNĒS _____

A) Write the Arabic equivalent of each of the following Roman numerals.

1. XXXIX   = _____
2. CCXLVI   = _____
3. DCCLXXII = _____
4. XCII   = _____
5. CXI   = _____

6. MDCCCXII   = _____
7. MCMLXXXIV = _____
8. MLXVI   = _____
9. MCMXLV   = _____
10. DCCCI   = _____

B) Below you will find a list of historical events. From the list of dates given, choose the correct year in which each event occurred. Write the Arabic numeral in the blank next to the event, then translate the Arabic numerals into Roman numerals

1941	1976
1776	1492
1969	117
1861	79

EVENT	YEAR IN ARABIC NUMERALS	YEAR IN ROMAN NUMERALS
1. Height of Roman Empire	_____	_____
2. Neil Armstrong: first man on the moon	_____	_____
3. Destruction of Pompeii	_____	_____
4. Pearl Harbor Day: entrance of United States into World War II	_____	_____
5. U.S. Bicentennial	_____	_____
6. Columbus lands in America	_____	_____
7. American Civil War	_____	_____
8. Declaration of Independence	_____	_____

LECTIO III

Establishing Some Ground Rules for Latin

Gender, Adjectives, Adjective Agreement

CLAUDIUS   CLAUDIA

CELER

I. EXPLICĀTIŌNĒS

GENDER: MASCULINE AND FEMININE NOUNS

In Latin, the endings of nouns generally tell us if the word is masculine or feminine. We have already seen this system applied to proper names. We know that Quintus, Publius, Claudius, and Celer are names of men and that Drūsīlla, Matella, and Claudia are names of women. The endings are an indication of the gender of the noun.

Although there are some exceptions, generally speaking, nouns that end in the letter a are called *first declension nouns*. Nouns that end in us or er are called *second declension nouns*. What is a *declension*? Simply a group of words that have the same type of ending. There are *five* declensions in Latin. In this book, we will limit our study to the first two.

DECLENSION	ENDING	GENDER
First Declension	-a	Feminine
Second Declension	-us or -er	Masculine

LATIN AND ENGLISH COMPARED: DETERMINING GENDER IN ENGLISH

In English, nouns that represent males are masculine.

> boy
> Paul
> actor

Nouns that represent females are feminine.

> girl
> Paula
> actress

Objects without sex are *neuter*, that is, they are neither masculine nor feminine.

> house
> book
> car

When we speak about any of these people or objects, we use the correct masculine, feminine, or neuter pronouns:

	NOUN	PRONOUN
The actor? <u>He</u>'s not really all that good.	actor = masculine	= he
Paula? <u>She</u> left early today—why do you ask?	Paula = feminine	= she
The house? <u>It</u> really isn't haunted, you know.	house = neuter	= it

LATIN AND ENGLISH COMPARED: DETERMINING GENDER IN LATIN

In Latin, the gender of a word is determined on a slightly different basis from English. A noun is masculine, feminine, or neuter according to what kind of ending it has. That means that in Latin, an object without sex may be masculine or feminine—as strange as that may seem—or neuter. Take a look at these examples:

mūr<u>us</u>	(wall)	(masculine)
lib<u>er</u>	(book)	(masculine)
port<u>a</u>	(door)	(feminine)
plūm<u>a</u>	(pen)	(feminine)

CONCLUSION

In Latin, gender depends on the ending the word carries.

Notā Bene: For the moment, we will concentrate our efforts on masculine and feminine nouns, because they make up the largest group. We will leave the study of neuter nouns to another time and place.

AN IMPORTANT EXCEPTION

There is one important exception to this rule of gender. In Latin, as in English, nouns that represent male beings are *always* masculine and those that represent female beings are *always* feminine. This is so even if the Latin endings of the words indicate otherwise.
The following words are masculine:

pu<u>er</u>	= boy
pat<u>er</u>	= father
Marc<u>us</u>	= Mark

The two nouns listed below are also masculine even though the endings of these words indicate that they should be feminine.

agricol<u>a</u>	= farmer	(masculine)
poēt<u>a</u>	= poet	(masculine)

NŌMEN _____

DIĒS _____

WHY ARE THESE WORDS WITH FEMININE ENDINGS MASCULINE?

Good question. We must remember that in Roman times, the social position of women was different from what it is today. Women were well respected and played an important role in most areas of Roman life, yet women were not farmers or poets. These were positions reserved for men only.

In the same way, the following word is feminine because it represents a female being (even though the -er ending seems to indicate that it is masculine).

mā<u>ter</u> = mother   (feminine)

Notā Bene: *Pater* and *māter* are third declension nouns.

We can summarize what we've been saying about gender in the following two rules.

CONCLUSIONS

1. Nouns of the first declension usually end in **-a.**
   They are generally feminine unless they refer to male beings.

2. Nouns of the second declension usually end in **-us** or **-er.**
   They are generally masculine unless they refer to female beings.

Here is a list of common Latin nouns. Indicate which are *masculine* and which are *feminine* by writing an M or an F in the spaces provided.

1. ____ **porta**	door		7. ____ **tabula**	notebook, writing tablet
2. ____ **fenestra**	window		8. ____ **papȳrus**	paper
3. ____ **mūrus**	wall		____ **charta**	paper
4. ____ **plūma**	pen		9. ____ **sella**	chair
5. ____ **liber**	book		____ **cathēdra**	chair
6. ____ **crēta**	chalk			

II. ADJECTIVES: WORDS THAT DESCRIBE

MASCULINE AND FEMININE ADJECTIVES

In Latin, an adjective that describes a masculine noun also takes a masculine ending and an adjective that describes a feminine noun takes a feminine ending.

NOTĀ BENE

Nouns NEVER change gender.

An adjective, however, MUST change its gender to match the noun it accompanies.

EXAMPLES:

Quintus est magnus.	Matella non est magna.	Porta est ūmida.
Quintus is big.	Matella is not big.	The door is wet.

Be careful about this one:

Liber est optimus.
The book is very good.

And this one:

Agricola (m.) est fīdus.
The farmer is faithful.

The following list contains some common Latin adjectives in their masculine and feminine forms. Adjectives are always listed in a Latin dictionary *in the masculine form.*

ADJECTIVES

	MASCULINE	FEMININE	ENGLISH MEANING
1.	albus	alba	white
2.	bonus	bona	good
3.	clārus	clāra	bright, famous, clear
4.	contentus	contenta	satisfied
5.	fīdus	fīda	faithful
6.	laetus	laeta	happy
7.	lātus	lāta	wide, broad
8.	longus	longa	long
9.	magnus	magna	big

10.	malus	mala	bad
11.	novus	nova	new
12.	optimus	optima	very good, best
13.	parātus	parāta	ready
14.	parvus	parva	little, small
15.	Rōmānus	Rōmāna	Roman
16.	ūmidus	ūmida	wet, moist

NOTĀ BENE

Look at the last two sentences in the examples given and their English translations. Since Latin, unlike English, has no articles (noun determiners), the words *a*, *an*, and *the* do not exist in Latin.

Therefore the word *liber* can mean: a) book
b) a book
c) the book

The word *agricola* can mean: a) farmer
b) a farmer
c) the farmer

In translating from Latin to English, you will have to supply the noun determiners yourself. Practice on these sentences.

1. Cathēdra est parva.

_____

2. Liber est ūmidus.

_____

3. Tabula nōn est parāta.

_____

4. Quintus est parātus.

_____

5. Charta est nova.

_____

6. Sella est alba.

_____

Index Verbōrum

AMĪCUS

AMĪCA

Nouns

agricola (m.) farmer
amīcus (male) friend
amīca (female) friend

asinus donkey
cibus food
culīna kitchen
discipulus (male) student
discipula (female) student
equus horse

EQUUS

ASINUS

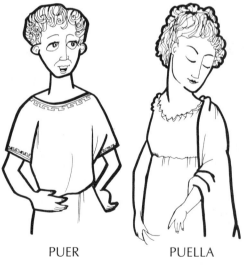

PUER

PUELLA

familia family
gallus rooster
hortus garden
lūna moon
magister teacher
poēta (m.) poet
puella girl
puer boy

rāna frog
schola school
taurus bull
via road, way

RĀNA

NŌMEN _____

DIĒS _____

_____ III. EXERCITĀTIŌNĒS _____

In the Latin sentences below, write an M or an F in the blank immediately *after* the number to indicate whether the *noun* of that sentence is masculine or feminine. (The blank *before* each number will be used in a later exercise.) Supply the correct ending for the adjective, then translate the sentence into GOOD English. Be sure to study the examples before you begin.

A) EXAMPLE: _____ **a)** __F__ Porta est magn __a__ .

The door is big.

_____ **b)** __F__ Porta alb __a__ est magn __a__.

The white door is big.

___ **1.** _____ Publius est content _____ .

_____

___ **2.** _____ Drūsīlla est content _____ .

_____

___ **3.** _____ Liber est optim _____ .

_____

___ **4.** _____ Mūrus est parv _____ .

_____

___ **5.** _____ Discipulus est clār _____ . (Two translations, please.)

_____

_____

___ **6.** _____ Taurus magn _____ est mal _____ .

_____

___ **7.** _____ Poēta est bon _____. (Be careful!)

_____

___ **8.** _____ Fenestra est lāt _____ .

_____

___ **9.** _____ Cibus est parāt _____ et optim _____ (et = and.)

_____

___ **10.** _____ Agricola content _____ est laet _____ .

_____

MAGNUS

PARVUS

Adjectives describe.

PLAY THE ESTNE GAME

One student is chosen as the priest or priestess who has all the knowledge. He or she chooses a Latin word from a category (nouns, verbs, adjectives, etc.) but does not reveal it to the class.

If the category is adjectives, students in the class raise their hands and in turn ask:

"ESTNE ALBUS, ALBA?" (Is it "albus, alba?")

The priest or priestess answers:

"MINIMĒ, NÔN EST ALBUS, ALBA." (No, it is not "albus, alba.")

When the correct answer is guessed, the response is:

"ITA, EST ŪMIDUS, ŪMIDA." (Yes, it is "ūmidus, ūmida.")

The student who guessed correctly replaces the priest or priestess and chooses a new word.

_____ **IV. ANALYSIS EXERCISE** _____

> **ANALYSIS QUESTION**
>
> **Where is an adjective placed in a Latin sentence?**

A) Do the following exercises.

1. Copy the two example sentences and their translations from the previous exercise in the spaces below.

    a) Latin: _____

    English: _____

    b) Latin: _____

    English: _____

2. Circle all of the adjectives (both English and Latin) in the sentences above. There are six of them in all.

3. Draw a box around each noun (both English and Latin) in the sentences above. There are four of them.

Now look at the nouns and adjectives in the sentences you wrote and where those nouns and adjectives are placed in relation to each other. Answer the following questions by circling the entire correct answer (not just the letter, please).

4. In Latin sentence *a* the adjective is
    a) on the same side of the verb as the noun.
    b) on the other side of the verb from the noun.

5. In English sentence *a* the adjective is
    a) on the same side of the verb as the noun.
    b) on the other side of the verb from the noun.

6. In Latin sentence *b* the first adjective is
   a) on the same side of the verb as the noun.
   b) on the other side of the verb from the noun.

   And the second adjective is

   a) on the same side of the verb as the noun.
   b) on the other side of the verb from the noun.

7. In English sentence *b* the first adjective is
   a) on the same side of the verb as the noun.
   b) on the other side of the verb from the noun.

   And the second adjective is

   a) on the same side of the verb as the noun.
   b) on the other side of the verb from the noun.

Notā Bene

An adjective which is joined directly to the noun it describes is known as an **attributive adjective,** because it describes immediately an *attribute* or *characteristic* of that noun.

An adjective that is separated from the noun it describes by a verb is known as a **predicate adjective,** because it is *part of the predicate* of the sentence.

---

8. Write the six adjectives from model sentences *a* and *b* below and indicate if they are attributive or predicate adjectives.

		ADJECTIVE	TYPE
a)	Latin:	_____	_____
	English:	_____	_____
b)	Latin:	_____	_____
		_____	_____
	English:	_____	_____
		_____	_____

9. Now look at Latin sentence *b*. The attributive adjective *alba* appears

    _____ the noun it describes.
    (IN FRONT OF/AFTER)

10. Look at English sentence *b*. The attributive adjective *white* appears

    _____ the noun it describes.
    (IN FRONT OF/AFTER)

From questions 9 and 10 above, we can make a very important generalization about Latin and English adjectives and their placement in a sentence. Draw your own conclusions by completing the sentences below with the words *before* or *after*.

CONCLUSIONS

1. *In English*, attributive adjectives are generally placed _____ the nouns they describe.

    white door   big girl   happy student

2. *In Latin*, attributive adjectives are generally placed _____ the nouns they describe.

    porta alba   puella magna   discipulus laetus

3. *In both English and Latin*, predicate adjectives are generally placed

    _____ the verb of the sentence.

NOTĀ BENE

There are some exceptions to this last rule, but in this book, we will always assume that Latin adjectives come *after* the noun unless told otherwise.

B) Go back to Exercise III on page XXXV and decide whether each adjective is an **attributive** or a **predicate** adjective. Indicate your answer (with an *A* or a *P*) in the blanks to the left of the number of each sentence. Be careful! If there are two or three adjectives, you will have two or three answers.

NŌMEN _____

DIĒS _____

LATIN ORDER   ENGLISH ORDER

C) Follow the directions carefully to complete this exercise correctly.

Step 1: Write four *different* masculine nouns and four *different* feminine nouns in the blank spaces below. Choose your nouns from the Index Verbōrum on page XXXIV.

Step 2: Now choose an adjective from the list on pages XXXII and XXXIII to describe each of your nouns. Be sure that the endings of your adjectives agree with the nouns they describe.

Step 3: Translate your nouns and adjectives into English.

MASCULINE NOUNS	ADJECTIVES	ENGLISH TRANSLATION
1. _____	_____	_____
2. _____	_____	_____
3. _____	_____	_____
4. _____	_____	_____

FEMININE NOUNS	ADJECTIVES	ENGLISH TRANSLATION
1. _____	_____	_____
2. _____	_____	_____
3. _____	_____	_____
4. _____	_____	_____

LECTIO IV

More Information about Latin

Word Order, Inflection, Nominative

and Accusative Cases

LATIN WORD ORDER

If you look at the Latin sentences on page XXXV, you will notice that they all contain the Latin word *est* (*is*). Latin sentences that contain *est* often follow an order similar to that of English.

EXAMPLES:

1. Claudius est puer.
   Claudius is a boy.

2. Marcia est puella.
   Marcia is a girl.

3. Rufus est discipulus.
   Rufus is the student.

In other Latin sentences, however, the order of the words is usually different from that of English. In a typical Latin sentence, the verb comes last.

EXAMPLES:

1. Claudius Marciam videt.
   Claudius sees Marcia.

2. Marcia Claudium et Caecilium nōn pulsat.
   Marcia does not hit Claudius and Caecilius.

LATIN: AN INFLECTED LANGUAGE

SUBJECT VERSUS OBJECT = NOMINATIVE VERSUS ACCUSATIVE

NOTĀ BENE

The **subject** of a sentence is the person or thing that performs the action of the verb.

Claudia hits a friend.

Claudia is the **subject** because Claudia does the hitting.

NOTĂ BENE

The **direct object** of a sentence is the person or thing that is receiving the action of the verb.

Claudia hits a friend.

Friend is the **direct object** because the friend is being hit (receiving the action of hitting).

In Latin, you can tell the *function* of a word in the sentence (for example, whether it is the subject or the object) by the type of ending it carries.

Words that are *subjects* have **nominative** case endings.

Words that are *direct objects* have **accusative** case endings.

These endings are called **inflections.** Any language that has case endings is an **inflected** language. (Later, we will take a look at English to see if it, too, is an **inflected** language.)

In Latin, the inflections (or endings) are slightly different for masculine and feminine nouns. Notice, however, that the accusative endings *all* have a final **m.** A word ending in **-m** is generally the direct object of a sentence.

Look at the chart below and notice what happens to a word when it moves from the subject slot to the direct object slot in Latin.

When a noun is a subject, it has a nominative case ending.		When a noun is a direct object, it has an accusative case ending.
NOUN/ENDING		NOUN/ENDING
fem.	puella	becomes	puellam
	-a		-am
masc.	mūrus	becomes	mūrum
	-us		-um
	liber	becomes	librum
	-er		-rum

Now look at the Latin translation of our model sentence about Claudia and her friend. Pay close attention to the **nominative** and **accusative** endings. (Vocabulary: *amīcus* = (male) friend, *pulsat* = he, she, it hits)

Claudia amīcum pulsat.

Notā Bene: It is customary to introduce new vocabulary nouns in the nominative case. All Latin dictionaries list words in this way.

Since it is the endings of the words that tell us what their functions are in the sentence (and not the order of the words in the sentence), can you write the Latin sentence above *four different ways* without changing its meaning?

(This can be done just by changing the order of the words but not their endings. Remember, if you change the endings, you also change the meaning! If you change only the order of the words in the sentence, the meaning stays the same. Of course, in this exercise you will have to move the verb from its customary position.)

_____

_____

_____

_____

Let's summarize what we have just learned. Fill in the blanks with the correct response.

CONCLUSIONS

1. **SUBJECTS:**

   Words that are *subjects* have _____ case endings.

   Words that are *subjects* _____ the action of the verb.
   (PERFORM/RECEIVE)

2. **DIRECT OBJECTS:**

   Words that are *direct objects* have _____ case endings.

   Words that are *direct objects* _____ the action of the verb.
   (PERFORM/RECEIVE)

3. Look at the list of *accusative* case endings. What one letter do we *always* find in both the masculine and feminine forms?

   The letter _____ .

   This letter is characteristic of the accusative case.

4. A language is said to be _____ when it has case endings.

Now do the Analysis Exercise on the next page to prove to yourself that you understand the difference between **nominative** and **accusative** and that you have learned something about Latin word order.

DID YOU KNOW . . . ?

Slavery was a common practice in ancient Rome and was a rather complicated institution. It was most often the price paid for losing a war. In addition, those who could not pay their taxes were often sold on the block as slaves for the amount that they owed the tax collector. Poor people sometimes sold themselves into slavery as a means of survival.

Some of the very wealthy owned many thousands of slaves, but even those of modest means might own one or two. Prices for slaves ranged from a few dollars to several thousands of dollars. Greek slaves were especially prized because they were considered to be intelligent and were generally well educated.

Although a master had complete authority of life and death over his slaves—and for that matter, over the other members of his family, including his wife—custom, religion, and public opinion usually prevailed to prevent frequent gross abuses of life and limb.

NŌMEN_____

DIĒS_____

I. ANALYSIS EXERCISE

ANALYSIS QUESTION

In Latin, is word order as important to meaning as it is in English?

Read the sentence below. Then answer the questions about the sentence by filling in the blanks or circling the correct response.

Claudiam amīcus pulsat.

_____

1. Who is hitting whom?

   _____

2. How do you know?

   _____

3. What does the **-am** ending on Claudia's name indicate? (*Two* things, please.)

   _____

4. What is the correct English translation of the word *Claudiam*?

   _____

5. What does the **-us** ending on *amīcus* indicate? (*Two* things, please.)

   _____

6. Write the translation of the Latin sentence in the blank space under it.

7. Can you write the English sentence a different way (using the same words) without changing the meaning?
   a)   b)

8. Can you write the Latin sentence *four different* ways (using the same words) without changing its meaning?

_____

_____

_____

_____

9. Copy the Analysis Question in the space below:

_____

10. Now answer the Analysis Question in your own words.

_____

_____

_____

_____ II. EXERCITĀTIŌNĒS _____

A) Up to this point, we have gathered quite a bit of information about Latin and how it works. Now we can begin analyzing Latin words according to the five different categories that we have studied.

NOTĀ BENE	
If you want to know about	**Ask yourself this question**
1. a part of speech:	Is the word a **noun**, a **verb**, or an **adjective**?
2. a declension:	If the word is a noun or an adjective, is it of the first declension (ending in **-a**) or of the second declension (ending in **-us** or **-er**)?
3. a case:	Is the word **nominative** or **accusative**?
4. a gender:	Is the word **masculine** or **feminine**?
5. a function:	Is the word the **subject** or the **direct object** of the sentence?

NŌMEN ______________________

DIĒS ______________________

B) Fill in the proper responses required in the exercise that follows. Be sure to consult the list in the *Notā Bene* on page XLVII. Do not abbreviate your answers, please.

1. bonus ______________________ (part of speech)

2. servum ______________________ (case)

3. servus ______________________ (function)

4. parvam ______________________ (gender)

5. puellam ______________________ (case)

6. pulsat ______________________ (part of speech)

7. cibus ______________________ (part of speech)

8. agricola ______________________ (gender)

9. librum ______________________ (function)

10. discipula ______________________ (declension)

11. est ______________________ (part of speech)

12. Claudius ______________________ (case)

13. familiam ______________________ (case)

14. familiam ______________________ (declension)

DID YOU KNOW . . . ?

Women held a respected place in Roman society. Unlike their Greek counterparts, Roman women were relatively liberated. The wealthy had slaves to attend to the daily chores and although they were responsible for the general management of the household, they also had time to visit with friends, go shopping, attend parties, games, performances, and even political gatherings with their husbands.

By age 14, when their brothers were attending classes at a school, girls were expected to be married and tending the household. Some families, however, did encourage their daughters to study and to engage in intellectual pursuits. Husbands for wealthy girls were often chosen for the political or social advantage they afforded, but the lower classes most often married for reasons of mutual affection.

C) Read the following short Latin story about Lūcius and Portia. It has been written with the vocabulary that you have studied so far in this book plus a few new words. Check the vocabulary list below for the words that you do not know.

INDEX VERBŌRUM

NOUNS

aqua water
lectus bed
puer, puerum boy
serva female slave, servant

servus male slave, servant
terra earth, land, soil
tunica tunic
urna vase

VERBS

clāmat (he, she, it) calls
est (he, she, it) is
  (does not take a direct object)
lacrimat (he, she, it) cries, weeps
habet (he, she, it) has (takes a
  direct object)

monet (he, she, it) warns or
  advises
pulsat (he, she, it) hits
tenet (he, she, it) holds
videt (he, she, it) sees

ADJECTIVES

irātus, irāta angry

stultus, stulta silly, foolish

OTHER

et and
etiam also, likewise, still
hodiē today
in casā in the house
in hortō in the garden

iterum again
nōn not (usually precedes the verb)
nunc now
sed but
ubi? where?

FĀBULA

Portia Lūcium Clāmat

Lūcius est puer Rōmānus. Discipulus bonus est et clārus etiam est.

Portia est puella Rōmāna. Portia est laeta et contenta. Lūcius est parvus sed Portia nōn parva est. Portia magna est.

Lūcius hodiē est in culīnā. Urna magna etiam in culīnā est. In hortō est Portia. Familia in casā nōn est. Portia urnam magnam videt sed urna aquam nōn habet. Portia contenta nōn est.

Portia servam novam clāmat. Ubi est aqua? Serva est fīda. Nunc urna magna aquam iterum habet et Portia contenta est. Portia urnam tenet et Lūcium clāmat. Portia parāta est.

Nunc, Lūcius est in hortō et urna aquam nōn habet. Tunica est ūmida. Lūcius est ūmidus. Terra est ūmida. Lūcius īrātus est. Lūcius Portiam pulsat et servam monet! Serva nova nōn est laeta et Portia lacrimat! Lūcius ūmidus et stultus est sed etiam est contentus.

TRANSLĀTIO

Now translate the story about Lūcius and Portia into GOOD English.

_____
_____
_____
_____
_____
_____
_____
_____
_____
_____
_____
_____
_____
_____
_____
_____
_____
_____
_____
_____
_____
_____
_____
_____
_____
_____
_____
_____

Lūcius est ūmidus et īrātus.

Did you ever wonder why **September, October, November,** and **December** are the 9th, 10th, 11th, and 12th months of the year instead of the 7th, 8th, 9th, and 10th months of the year as their names would suggest?

Until Julius Caesar reformed the calendar in the year 46 B.C. by adopting the more accurate Egyptian calendar, the Roman year used to begin with the month of March and end with the month of February. Thus, according to the old Roman calendar, September through December were indeed the months 7 through 10 respectively.

Julius Caesar, however, in his revised "Julian" calendar (named after himself) began the new year with the month of January. This shifted the months of September through December to the 9th through 12th positions respectively, although their names were not altered to reflect the change. Our modern calendar is known as the Gregorian calendar because it was changed slightly by Pope Gregory XIII in 1582 to make it even more accurate. Otherwise, we continue to use a calendar that is exactly like the one established by Julius Caesar's astronomers in the first century B.C.!

NŌMEN _____

DIĒS _____

_____ III. EXERCITĀTIŌNĒS _____

A) The *nominative case* endings indicate that a word is the subject of a sentence. The *accusative case* endings indicate that the word is the direct object of the sentence. Keeping this in mind, translate the following Latin sentences into English.

1. Marcus discipulum videt. _____

2. Discipulus Marcum monet. _____

3. Drūsīlla gallum habet. _____

4. Poēta puellam videt. _____

5. Taurum Quintus clāmat. _____

6. Equum magister habet. _____

7. Asinus cibum videt. _____

8. Monet Iūliam amīcus. _____

9. Tunicam puella tenet. _____

10. Puer rānam videt. _____

11. Agricola tabulam habet. _____

12. Videt Claudius culīnam. _____

Nominative or Accusative?

B) Below and on the next page are some English sentences. Underline the **subject** of each English sentence *once* and the **direct object** of each English sentence *twice*. Then consult the chart on page XLIV and supply the proper endings for the nouns in the Latin sentences (nominative or accusative).

EXAMPLES: 1.   Rufus sees the notebook.

Ruf __us__ tabul __am__ videt.

EXAMPLES: 2.   The girl has the paper.

Papȳr __um__ puell __a__ habet.

1. The student has a donkey.

   Discipul _____ asin _____ habet.

2. The teacher has a student.

   Magist _____ discipul _____ habet.

3. The frog sees the rooster.

   Gall _____ rān _____ videt.

4. A friend has the horse.

   Amīc _____ equ _____ habet.

5. The boy has the tunic.

   Pu _____ tunic _____ habet.

6. The vase has water (in it).

   Urn _____ aqu _____ habet.

7. The slave hits the bed.

   Lect _____ serv _____ pulsat.

8. Claudia has the pen and the book.

   Habet Claudi _____ plūm _____ et lib _____ .

9. The student doesn't call the teacher.

   Discipul _____ magist _____ nōn clāmat.

ROMAN LEGIONNAIRE

NOTĀ BENE

You have learned that adjectives agree in gender with the nouns they describe (see page XXXII). They also agree in *case* (nominative, accusative).

C) After doing exercise B, try your hand at these sentences that contain not only nouns, but adjectives, too. Remember, since an adjective agrees in **gender** and **case** with the noun it describes, then if the noun is accusative, the adjective that describes it will also be accusative. Before you start, underline the **subject** and its **adjective(s)** once, and the **direct object** and its **adjective(s)** twice.

1. The bright student doesn't have a good teacher.

   Discipul _____ clār _____ magistr _____ bon _____ nōn habet.

2. The new servant warns the foolish girl.

   Puell _____ stult _____ serv _____ nov _____ monet.

3. The famous Roman sees the long, wide road.

   Rōmān _____ clār _____ vi _____ long _____ et lāt_____ videt.

IV. ANALYSIS EXERCISE

MORE ON WORD ORDER

ANALYSIS QUESTION

What is "typical" English word order?
What is "typical" Latin word order?

Refer to Exercise III, parts B and C, on pages LII–LIV, to answer the following questions. Write the letter of the correct response in the blank on the left.

_____ 1. The Latin word *videt* means
   a) is   b) was   c) sees   d) has

_____ 2. The Latin word *habet* means
   a) is   b) was   c) sees   d) has

_____ 3. *Videt* and *habet* are
   a) nouns   b) verbs   c) adjectives

_____ 4. With the exception of the verb *est* (*is*), the normal position for verbs in a Latin sentence is

      a) first   **b)** second   **c)** next-to-last   **d)** last

_____ 5. In which Latin sentence does the verb *not* appear in its normal Latin position? The number of that sentence is

_____ 6. In each of the twelve English sentences (parts B and C), the subject of the sentence comes

      a) before the verb   **b)** after the verb

_____ 7. In each of the twelve English sentences, the direct object of the sentence comes

      a) before the verb   **b)** after the verb

_____ 8. In each of the twelve English sentences, the verb comes

      a) before the subject
      b) after the direct object
      c) between the subject and the object

CONCLUSION NO. 1

Based on our observations in Questions 6, 7, and 8 above, we can make this statement (answer *true* or *false*):

_____ **There seems to be a definite pattern to the word order of an English sentence (subject-verb-object).**

Now, let's continue with our analysis.

_____ 9. Looking over the twelve Latin sentences, the verb _____ comes last.
    a) always   **b)** usually   **c)** sometimes   **d)** never

_____ 10. In the twelve Latin sentences, the direct object is placed before the subject in _____ sentences.
    a) three   **b)** six   **c)** seven   **d)** eight

11. Write down the number of each sentence in which the direct object precedes the subject in Latin.

_____

12. Write down the number of each sentence in which the direct object immediately follows the subject in Latin.

_____

CONCLUSION NO. 2

Based on our observations in Questions 9, 10, and 11, we can make this statement (fill in the blank):

Word order in Latin is not as important as it is in English, because

_____ of each Latin noun tells us what its function is in the sentence.

    1. the accent
    2. the first letter
    3. the case ending

ANALYSIS QUESTIONS

Copy the two Analysis Questions from the beginning of this exercise here:

1. _____

2. _____

ANALYSIS ANSWERS

In your own words, answer the two questions above.

1. _____

2. _____

 _____

 _____

Latin word order is flexible.

_____ V. EXERCITĀTIŌNĒS _____

NOMINATIVE AND ACCUSATIVE

A) Using what you have learned about subjects and direct objects so far, supply the correct endings (nominative or accusative) for the nouns in the following Latin sentences. *Be careful! Each sentence has to make sense.* One of the sentences below can be answered in more than one way. When you find it, mark it with a star. When you have added the correct endings, translate each sentence into GOOD English.

EXAMPLES: Ruf __us__ tabul __am__ magn __am__ videt.
_Rufus sees the big notebook._____

Habet papȳr __um__ Matell __a_____ .
_Matella has the paper._____

1. Equ _____ port _____ videt.

   _____

2. Puell _____ plūm _____ habet.

   _____

3. Magist _____ chart _____ alb _____ videt.

   _____

4. Tabul _____ bon _____ puell _____ habet.

   _____

5. Claudi _____ Quint _____ videt.

   _____

   _____

6. Habet papȳr _____ puell _____ .

   _____

7. Did you remember to mark with a star the sentence that could have more than one answer?

B) A lot of looking is going on in the exercise below. In each instance, the *subject* of the sentence does the seeing and the *direct object* gets seen. Translate each sentence into Latin, making sure that both the subject and the direct object have the proper endings. Be sure to put the verb last.

> **EXAMPLE:** Publius sees Drūsīlla.
>
> _____Publius Drūsīllam videt._____

1. The donkey sees a girl.

   _____

2. The student sees the teacher.

   _____

3. The teacher sees the student, also.

   _____

4. Now the boy sees a little cottage.

   _____

5. The girl sees the book and the pen.

   _____

6. Emily sees a friend. (What is the Latin equivalent of "Emily"?)

   _____

C) The following sentences contain words that we have not studied in Latin. We will not be translating them, however, but identifying the *functions* of the underlined words in each sentence. Study each underlined word and decide whether that word is the subject or the direct object of the sentence. Then, in the space provided, write the *case* that you would use to translate that word into Latin. Please do not abbreviate your answers.

1. John and his <u>parents</u> arrived from Chicago yesterday.

   (_____)

2. Have you ever seen the Leaning <u>Tower</u> of Pisa?

(_____)

3. The car that his <u>uncle</u> bought fell into the ditch.

(_____)

4. Political <u>problems</u> sometimes are the cause of inflation.

(_____)

5. The Dodgers soundly defeated the <u>Yankees</u> yesterday.

(_____)

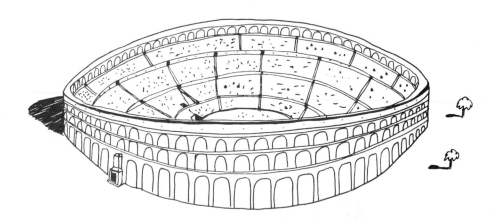

THE COLOSSEUM

The majestic remains of the Colosseum in the heart of modern Rome serve as an awe-inspiring reminder of the time of the Roman emperors. For 500 years, this huge arena was the scene of great spectacles—many of them bloody and violent—that served as "entertainment" for the masses. Covering six acres, it had a seating capacity for 45,000 spectators on marble or wooden benches with additional standing room for 5,000 more! There were 76 entranceways called *vomitoriae* and canvas runners that could be quickly pulled into place to protect the entire area from rain or the hot afternoon sun, a forerunner of our modern-day domed stadiums.

Beneath the oval floor of the arena, there was a maze of corridors and underground cells where animals as well as criminals, prisoners of war, and gladiators were kept before being taken to their deaths in the arena above. The floor of the arena was often flooded to provide an artificial sea for spectacular naval battles between opposing teams.

_____ **VI. ANALYSIS EXERCISE** _____

ANALYSIS QUESTION

Well?! Is English an inflected language like Latin or not?

A)   Turn to page XLVI and, in the space below, copy the first question of the Analysis Exercise that appears on that page. Make sure that you copy the *question*, not the answer.

_____

This English sentence is composed of four words: a subject, a verb form composed of *two* words, and a direct object (in that order).

1.   Write the verb form (both words) in the spaces below.

_____   _____

2.   Write the word that is the *subject* of the sentence on this line.

_____

3.   Write the word that is the direct object of the sentence on the line below.

_____

4.   Now compare the second and third answers. Both of these words (although they are spelled differently) mean the same thing: "What person?" In fact, you would be asking the same question if you said: "*What person* is hitting *what person?*"

   a)   What is the last letter of the *direct object* word?

_____

   b)   What case in Latin is characterized by this letter?

_____

   c)   When this case is used in Latin, it indicates that the word is (circle one)

      the subject of a sentence   the direct object of a sentence

---

CONCLUSION NO. 1

Explain now, in your own words, why the two words in answers 2 and 3 are spelled differently even though they mean the same thing.

If you can't answer this question yet, read Conclusion No. 2 first and then come back to this question.

_____

_____

CONCLUSION NO. 2

When we want to use a word that means "What person?" as the *direct object* of a sentence, we write:

_____

When we want to use a word that means "What person?" as the *subject* of a sentence, we write:

_____

The different endings of these two similar words prove that English _____ an inflected language.
(IS/IS NOT)

B) Consider these two groups of sentences

GROUP I	GROUP II
a) I see Mary.	Mary sees me.
b) He sees Mary.	Mary sees him.
c) They see Mary.	Mary sees them.
d) She sees Mary.	Mary sees her.
e) We see Mary.	Mary sees us.
f) You see Mary.	Mary sees you.

1. According to what we've already learned about the predictability of English word order (see page LVII), the word **before** the verb in each of the sentences is the subject and the word **after** the verb is the direct object.

   Circle each subject and underline each direct object in both groups. There are twelve of each.

That should have been easy enough! Now, let's make some comparisons and observations. Follow the directions carefully. Choose the correct answer from those given and write it in the blank provided.

2. The sentences of Group II are _____ in meaning to their
(THE SAME/OPPOSITE)
counterparts in Group I.

3. Mary is the _____ of each sentence in Group I.
(SUBJECT/DIRECT OBJECT)

4. Mary is the _____ of each sentence in Group II.
(SUBJECT/DIRECT OBJECT)

5. The proper noun *Mary* _____ change its form when it
(DOES/DOES NOT)
moves from the subject slot to the direct object slot.

6. If I substitute *the cat* for *Mary* in each of the sentences on page LXII, the
word *cat* _____ change its form when it moves from the subject
(WILL/WILL NOT)
slot to the direct object slot.

> ## CONCLUSION No. 3
>
> Most nouns in English _____ change their form when they
> (SEEM TO/DO NOT SEEM TO)
> move from the subject slot to the direct object slot in a sentence.

OK, LET'S CONTINUE OUR ANALYSIS

Consider the 12 sentences in Groups I and II as six pairs of sentences. Look at the words that you circled in Group I and those that you underlined in Group II. Each of these words is a *pronoun*, that is, each is a word that *stands for a noun*. The word *pronoun* comes from two Latin words:

PRO = *for* and **NŌMEN** = _____.)

Therefore, a *pro-noun* is a word that *stands for the name* of a person, place, thing, or idea.

We can say "David sees Mary" or we can substitute the *pronouns* for David and Mary and say "He sees her." *David* and *Mary* are nouns. *He* and *her* are pronouns. Got that? OK. Then answer the questions that follow.

7. What happens to *I* when it moves from the subject slot to the direct object slot?

    It changes from _____ to _____ .

8. What happens to *he* when it moves from the subject slot to the direct object slot?

    It changes from _____ to _____ .

9. What happens to *they* when it moves from the subject slot to the direct object slot?

    It changes from _____ to _____ .

NOTĀ BENE

Notice that each of the direct object forms that we've been talking about here contains the same letter. That letter is _____ . We have already learned that in Latin this letter is typical of the _____ case and usually indicates that the word is the _____ of the sentence. Do you think there might be a connection here between Latin and English?

DID YOU KNOW . . . ?

The custom of carrying the bride over the threshold on her wedding day originated with the Romans. As a symbol of future plenty, well-wishers anointed the doorway of the new couple's home with oils and fats. Of course, it would have been a bad omen for the couple to slip and fall on their wedding day. To ensure that such a luckless mishap would not happen, the bridegroom lifted his bride and carried her safely inside.

The traditional wedding band also originated with the Romans who believed that a vein extended from the third finger of the left hand directly to the heart. It became customary at Roman wedding ceremonies to place an iron band on the third finger to symbolize the "capture" of the loved one's heart. Of course, it is a custom that is still practiced today in one form or another in many countries throughout the world.

---

10. What happens to *she* when it moves from the subject slot to the direct object slot?

It changes from _____ to _____ .

11. What happens to *we* when it moves from the subject slot to the direct object slot?

It changes from _____ to _____ .

NOTĀ BENE

Do the direct object pronouns that we've been discussing in questions 10 and 11 follow the Latin accusative model and contain the letter *m*?

_____

---

12. What happens to *you* when it moves from the subject slot to the direct object slot?

You _____ .

CAN WE DRAW SOME FINAL CONCLUSIONS FROM ALL OF THIS NOW?

Use the information you have collected in this Analysis Exercise as well as what you already know about Latin to help you complete the following statements. Write the correct answer in the blank spaces.

CONCLUSION NO. 4

In English, a noun usually _____ a different form when it
(DOES HAVE/DOES NOT HAVE)
acts as a subject or as a direct object of a sentence.

In Latin, a noun usually _____ a different form when it is
(DOES HAVE/DOES NOT HAVE)
the subject or the direct object of the sentence.

Do the two statements above agree with what you learned in this chapter?

_____
(YES/NO)

ANALYSIS ANSWER

From the information contained in Conclusions 4 and 5 above, we can safely

say that English _____ an inflected language.
(IS/IS NOT)

We can further state that English _____ as highly inflected
(SEEMS TO BE/DOES NOT SEEM TO BE)
as Latin.

THISISANEXAMPLEOFROMANWRITING

Read the paragraph below. Although it may not seem like it at first glance, it is written in English!

WHENINROMEWRITEASTHEROMANSDO
THISISANEXAMPLEOFWHATOURWRITINGWOULDLOOKLIKETODAYIFWE
FOLLOWEDTHECUSTOMOFMOSTROMANSCRIBESDURINGTHEEARLYROMAN
EMPIRETHEYUSUALLYLEFTNOSPACESBETWEENWORDSSOITWASNOTALWAYS
IMMEDIATELYCLEARWHEREONEWORDENDEDANDANOTHERBEGANOFCOURSE
THEREWERENOPUNCTUATIONMARKSEITHERTOGUIDETHEREADERANDTOHELP
ASSEMBLETHEWORDSINTOMEANINGFULGROUPSISNTITTOOBADTHATWE
DIDNTWRITETHISWHOLETEXTBOOKINTHISTYPICALROMANMANNERITWOULD
HAVEBEENSOMUCHMOREAUTHENTIC

LECTIO V

More about Adjectives: Words That Describe

Adjective Placement, Adjective Agreement

There's more than one way to describe a dog!

Adjectives are words that describe nouns or pronouns. Words like *big*, *little*, *brown*, and *happy* are adjectives.

On page XXXII, we learned that Latin adjectives can be masculine or feminine depending on what kind of noun they modify. Complete the Analysis Exercise on the following pages to find out more about how adjectives behave in Latin (and in English).

_____ I. ANALYSIS EXERCISE _____

ANALYSIS QUESTION

Are there *any* rules for word order in Latin?

We have already seen that a typical Latin sentence puts the verb at the end. Consider the example sentence below, then answer the questions based on it by circling the entire answer or filling in the blanks.

EXAMPLE: Puer Rōmānus tabulam novam habet.

_____ The Roman boy has a new notebook (writing tablet). _____

1.   What are the Latin endings for the words *boy* and *Roman*?

_____ and _____

These endings indicate that these two words are (circle one in each group)

gender:	**a)** masculine	**b)** feminine
case:	**a)** nominative	**b)** accusative
function:	**a)** subject	**b)** direct object
declension:	**a)** first	**b)** second

2. What are the Latin endings for the words *tablet* and *new*?

    _____ and _____

    These endings indicate that these words are

    declension: gender: _____

                       case: _____

                       function: _____

                       declension: _____

3. Are the adjectives in this sentence attributive or predicate adjectives? (See *Notā Bene* on page XXXVIII.)

    _____

4. It would *not* be possible to translate the Latin sentence in our example as "The new boy has a Roman notebook," because
    a) *puer* is not the subject of the sentence.
    b) *new* must describe *notebook*. Because both of these words have feminine accusative endings in Latin.

5. Read and compare the two sentences below.
    a) Puer Rōmānus tabulam novam habet.
    b) Puer novam tabulam Rōmānus habet.

6. Is it possible to translate sentence 5b like this?
"The new boy has the Roman writing tablet."
a) yes   **b)** no

Why? (Circle all correct answers.)

a) because *novam* can modify *puer*.
b) because *novam* cannot modify *puer*.
c) because *Rōmānus* can modify *tabulam*.
d) because *Rōmānus* cannot modify *tabulam*.

7. Because the endings of adjectives tell us which nouns they modify, which of the two sentences in question 5 do you feel is less confusing?
    a) sentence "a"   **b)** sentence "b"

Can you state in your own words why you think so?

_____

> ## CONCLUSION
>
> Although subjects, objects, and even verbs can be moved about in a Latin sentence without changing the sentence's meaning, a noun and its modifying adjective most often
>
>   **a)** function as a unit.
>   **b)** function separately.
>
> Therefore a noun and its modifying adjective
>
>   **a)** will move together in a sentence.
>   **b)** can move independently in a sentence.

8. Could we rewrite the original Latin sentence like this without changing its meaning?

Habet puer Rōmānus tabulam novam.

a) yes   **b)** no

9. Which Latin sentence shows "typical" word order?
a) The original sentence in the example at the beginning of this Analysis Exercise.
b) The sentence in question 8.

10. Explain why you answered question 9 as you did. (State the rule that applies.)

_____

_____

ANALYSIS ANSWER

Because Latin is an inflected language, there is much flexibility in the order in which words can appear in a sentence. That's because we can depend on the endings of words to convey much of the meaning in a sentence.

1. In a Latin sentence, however, attributive adjectives generally

    _____ the nouns they describe.
    (PRECEDE/FOLLOW)

2. A noun and its modifying adjective most often function

    _____ and _____.
    (AS A UNIT/SEPARATELY)   (MUST MOVE TOGETHER/CAN MOVE INDEPENDENTLY)

3. In addition, in a typical Latin sentence, the verb usually appears

    _____ .
    (FIRST/LAST)

4. Because of all of the above statements, we can safely conclude that there

    _____ some rules that govern Latin word order, and
    (ARE/ARE NOT)

    that words _____ be placed in random order in a
               (CAN/CANNOT)

    Latin sentence.

_____ II. ANALYSIS EXERCISE _____

> ### ANALYSIS QUESTION
>
> **In what way does an adjective agree with the noun it describes?**

There are two adjectives in the example sentence below: *little* and *big*. They describe *girl* and *book*, respectively. Looking at the Latin translation, complete the following statements.

EXAMPLE: The little girl has a big book.
                 Puella parva librum magnum habet.

1. When a noun is feminine, the adjective that accompanies it is

    _____
                          (GENDER)
    In the blank below, write the feminine noun and its adjective (in Latin) as they appear in the example sentence.

    _____

2. When a noun is masculine, the adjective that accompanies it is

    _____
                          (GENDER)
    In the blank below, write the masculine noun and its adjective (in Latin) as they appear in the example sentence.

    _____

3. When a noun is in the nominative case, the adjective that accompanies it is

    in the _____ case.
    Write the nominative case ending (the ending only, please) that occurs in the Latin example sentence:

    _____

4. When a noun is in the accusative case, the adjective that accompanies it is in

the _____ case.

Write the two accusative case endings (endings only) that occur in the Latin example sentence.

_____

_____

ANALYSIS ANSWER

An adjective agrees in case and gender with the noun it modifies.

True or false: _____

_____ III. EXERCITĀTIŌNĒS _____

A) Translate each of the following sentences into GOOD English. All of the adjectives are in italics to help you spot them. Watch them change position as you translate from Latin to English. Pay attention to case endings to spot subjects and direct objects.

1. Publius equum *bonum* clāmat.

   _____

2. Familia *magna* casam *magnam* habet.

   _____

3. Lūnam *clāram* discipulus *Rōmānus* etiam videt.

   _____

4. Videt scholam *parvam* Cornēlia.

   _____

5. Nunc, puer *stultus* iterum tenet gallum *magnum* in hortō.

   _____

6. Asinus *contentus* nōn videt cibum et aquam.

   _____

7. Agricola *Rōmānus* sellam *novam* habet.

   _____

8. Ubi est discipulus *īrātus?*

   _____

9. Tullius terram *ūmidam* in hortō videt.

   _____

10. Amīcus *bonus* tunicam *longam* tenet.

    _____

B) This exercise has three parts. Follow the directions carefully.

   PART A

   First underline the adjective in each English expression, then translate each expression into Latin. Assume that each expression is the *subject* of a sentence. Therefore, you must use only *nominative case endings*.

   EXAMPLE: The <u>little</u> boy: ____Puer parvus____

   1. The large bull: _____

   2. A faithful servant: _____

   3. The good school: _____

   PART B

   Underline the adjective in each of the following English expressions, then translate the expression into Latin. Assume that each expression is the *direct object* of a sentence. Therefore, you must use only *accusative case endings*.

   EXAMPLE: The <u>little</u> girl: ____puellam parvam____

   1. The white door: _____

   2. The small vase: _____

   3. A very good teacher: _____

PART C

Now combine the subjects of Part A and the direct objects of Part B with the verbs given below to form complete Latin sentences. Match *subject 1* with *direct object 1* with *verb 1*, etc. Then translate your sentence into GOOD English. Be sure to use normal Latin word order.

EXAMPLE: (pulsat)

_____ Puer parvus puellam parvam pulsat. _____

_____ The little boy hits the little girl. _____

1. (videt)

_____

_____

2. (tenet)

_____

_____

3. (habet)

_____

_____

C)   Translate the following sentences into Latin. Be careful of case endings! The Latin verb is given in parentheses. Make sure that you place it correctly in the sentence.

1.   The cottage is (est) ready. Where is (est) the farmer?

_____

2.   The teacher has (habet) the small writing tablet.

_____

3.   The happy boy sees (videt) the happy girl again.

_____

4.   The foolish servant also has (habet) a long tunic.

_____

D) Look at the two groups of scrambled words below and follow the directions carefully.

    a) First, circle all the adjectives.

    b) Then unscramble the words so that they form a coherent and correct Latin sentence. Write the sentence on line 1.

    c) Write the sentence three other ways in Latin on lines 2, 3, 4. (You will have to move the verb from its usual last place.)

    d) Finally, translate your sentences into GOOD English on line 5.

habet/cibum/laeta/puella/bonum

    1. _____

    2. _____

    3. _____

    4. _____

    5. _____

magister/videt/Latīnum/Rōmānus/librum

    1. _____

    2. _____

    3. _____

    4. _____

    5. _____

E) Choose the word that completes each sentence. Be careful to choose the word that fits *grammatically*, applying what you have learned about agreement. Write the word in the space provided and translate the sentence into English.

    1. _____ servus pulsat.
         (RĀNA/LECTUM/PUELLA)

    _____

    2. _____ discipulum nōn monet.
         (MAGISTER/MAGISTRUM/SERVAM)

    _____

    3. Amīcus _____ puellam clāmat.
         (BONA/BONUS/DRŪSILLA)

    _____

LECTIO VI

A Day in the Life of Quintus Caecilius Fēlix

FĀBULA

Quintus Caecilius Fēlix in Scholā

1. Quintus est puer Rōmānus.
   Prōcērus, magnus, et formōsus est.

2. Trānio est paedagōgus.

3. Clēmens est capsārius.
   Trānio et Clēmens sunt servī Rōmānī.

4. Theodorus est grammaticus Graecus.
   Clārus, honestus, et iustus est Theodorus.

5. Hodiē, Quintus in scholā est.
   Grammaticus est fatīgātus
   sed Quintus fatīgātus nōn est.

6. Rāna etiam in scholā hodiē est.
   Quintus rānam videt. Parva rāna est.

7. Quintus Clēmentem videt.
Clēmens in hortum ambulat.
Urnam magnam portat.

8. Prope murum Clēmens urnam locat.
Aqua in urnā est. In aquam
Quintus rānam locat et urnam
locat prope Theodorum.

9. Nunc rāna in aquā est.
Quintus est contentus.
Rāna est contenta, sed . . .

10. Theodorus contentus nōn est.
Irātus est. Aquam amat sed
rānam in aquā nōn amat.

INDEX VERBŌRUM

NOUNS

capsārius   a slave who carried his young master's satchel to school.

grammaticus   a grammarian, secondary school teacher

paedagōgus   a slave who accompanied children to and from school and had charge of them at home

ADJECTIVES

fatīgātus, fatīgāta   weary, tired

formōsus, formōsa   beautiful, handsome

Graecus, Graeca   Greek

honestus, honesta   honored, honorable, respectable

iustus, iusta   just, fair

prōcērus, prōcēra   tall

VERBS

amat   (he, she, it) loves

ambulat   (he, she, it) walks

locat   (he, she, it) puts, places

portat   (he, she, it) carries

sunt   they are

OTHER

hodiē   today

in   (+ ablative) in

in   (+ accusative) into

ita   certainly (yes)

ita vērō   certainly! (yes!)

minimē   not at all (no)

nōn   not

prope   (+ accusative) next to, near (to)

NOTĀ BENE

Latin has no real equivalent for our English words *yes* and *no*. Instead of answering simply "yes" or "no" to a question, a speaker of Latin would have repeated the verb either affirmatively or negatively. The nearest translation is:

1.	Is he carrying the vase?	Portatne urnam?
	Yes.	Ita, portat.
	Yes, he is.	Ita, portat.
2.	Does he see?	Videtne?
	No.	Minimē, nōn videt.
	No, he doesn't.	Minimē, nōn videt.

The word vērō (truly) is an adverb. When it is used together with ita, it indicates emphasis.

3.	Does she like Mark?	Amatne Marcum?
	Yes!	Ita vērō, amat!
	Yes, she does!	Ita vērō, amat!

_____ I. EXERCITĀTIŌNĒS _____

A)   Tell whether each of the following statements is true or false according to the story about Quintus Caecilius Fēlix. Write *T* or *F* in the blanks on the left and be prepared to support your answer with specific passages from the story.

_____   **1.** Theodorus est puer Rōmānus.

_____

_____   **2.** Clēmens est servus Rōmānus.

_____

_____   **3.** Quintus prōcērus et formōsus est.

_____

_____   **4.** Trānio est paedagōgus.

_____

_____   **5.** Quintus rānam parvam videt.

_____

_____   **6.** In aquam Clēmens rānam locat.

_____

_____   **7.** Clēmens urnam portat.

_____

_____   **8.** In aquam Clēmentem Quintus locat.

_____

_____   **9.** Rāna contenta nōn est.

_____

_____   **10.** Theodorus contentus nōn est.

_____

B)   Now, rewrite each of the sentences you marked *false* so that each is a true statement according to the story. Write your answers in the spaces provided above and in Latin, naturally.

Notā Bene

THE MACRON AND THE LATIN WORD *IN*

Notice that the Latin word *in* changes its meaning slightly depending on the case of the noun that follows it.

IN + THE ABLATIVE CASE (*in hortō, in aquā*)
(IN + ABLATIVE = IN)

Although we have not studied the **ablative** case yet, you should know three things about it:

1. It is often used to show "place where" (that is, stationary location: *in* the house, *in* the garden, etc.).
2. At first glance, the feminine singular ending of the ablative case may *look* like the nominative case ending, but it's not the same at all. The nominative case ending is a *short* a; the ablative case ending is a *long* a and is written like this: ā. Don't forget to add the macron to the final *a* on all feminine words in the ablative case.
3. In the masculine singular, the ablative case ending is a *long* o and is written like this: ō.

IN + THE ACCUSATIVE CASE (in hortum, in aquam)
(IN + ACCUSATIVE = INTO)

The use of the *accusative* case after in changes its meaning to *into*. Compare the following:

FEMININE

1. Cornēlia in culīnā est. (in + ablative)
   Cornēlia is <u>in</u> the kitchen.

2. Cornēlia pūpam (doll) in urn**am** locat. (in + accusative)
   Cornēlia puts the doll in<u>(to)</u> the vase.

MASCULINE

1. Titus in hortō est. (<u>in</u> + ablative)
   Titus is <u>in</u> the garden.

2. Titus in hort**um** ambulat. (<u>in</u> + accusative)
   Titus walks <u>into</u> the garden.

_____ II. ANALYSIS EXERCISE _____

> ### ANALYSIS QUESTION
>
> **Does the subject of a sentence always have to be present, or are there other ways to indicate who is performing the action of the sentence?**

A) How well did you really understand the story about Quintus? Using your knowledge of Latin, answer the following questions by writing the correct response or circling the correct answer and discover more information about how Latin works.

1. What is the meaning of the verb *est*? Look at the *Index Verbōrum* on page XLIX, to be sure that you have the *entire* meaning, then write your answer in the blank below.

   _____

2. We have learned that the verb *est* does not take a direct object. Notice that there is no accusative case in the simple sentences below that contain *est*. How do we translate the following two sentences?

   Quintus est puer. _____

   Quintus est formōsus. _____

3. What is the subject of each of the sentences on the preceding page?

_____

4. Now look at these two sentences.

   Quintus est puer.
   Formōsus est.

The subject of the first sentence is still *Quintus*, but what is the subject of the second sentence? To answer this question, go back to Question 1 of this exercise, and in the space below, write in the *entire* meaning of the verb *est*.

_____

Since there are *three* choices for a subject here, which *one* is most appropriate when we are talking about Quintus? Write your answer below.

_____

Now can you translate the original sentence?

   Formōsus est. _____

5. What if we change the sentences to read like this?

   Cornēlia est puella.
   Formōsā est.

What is the subject of the first sentence above?

_____

How would you translate both sentences? Be careful of your choice of adjective this time!

_____

==

DID YOU KNOW . . . ?

The ancient Romans were much more knowledgeable about medicine than is commonly thought. Roman physicians knew about and prescribed a wide variety of medications for their patients' ills. Surgeons knew how to give blood transfusions and were able to perform major surgery. They closed their incisions with needle and thread and covered them with clean bandages to speed healing. Roman doctors were also aware of the value of inoculations to prevent the spread of disease.

==

6. Finally, look at these next two sentences and answer the questions about them before drawing some new conclusions about subjects, objects, and the importance of word endings in Latin.

Cornēlia librum tenet.
Formōsus est.

a) What is the subject of the first sentence? _____

b) What is the direct object of the first sentence? _____

c) What is the gender of the subject? _____

d) What is the gender of the direct object? _____

e) What is the gender of the adjective in the second sentence?

_____

f) Can a masculine adjective describe a feminine noun?

_____

g) Well then, what word does *formōsus* describe, *Cornēlia* or *liber*?

_____

h) Translate the two sentences in the space below.

_____

ANALYSIS ANSWER

The subject of a Latin sentence _____ always have to be
(DOES/DOES NOT)
present in the form of a noun or a pronoun.

The subject of a sentence _____ be indicated by the
(CAN/CANNOT)
full meaning of the verb.

If it is not clear exactly what word is really the subject, we can look to other

clues in the sentence to help us, like the ending on the _____.
(PART OF SPEECH)

B) Translate the following sentences into GOOD English. Be careful of the endings on the adjectives. They tell you which noun the adjective describes.

1. Serva asinum album videt. Fīda et bona est.

_____

2. Puer familiam magnam habet. Laeta est.

_____

3. Urnam parvam Marcellus tenet. Alba est sed nova nōn est.

_____

_____

4. Magister prope casam hodiē est. Prōcērus est.

_____

5. Antōnia amīcum clāmat. Rōmānus est.

_____

6. Claudius tunicam portat. Parva est.

_____

7. Magister familiam novam amat. Honesta et iusta est.

_____

_____

8. Semprōnia in scholā iterum nōn est. Stulta est.

_____

9. Horātia librum bonum habet. Bonus est.

_____

10. Caecilius in scholā nunc est. Formōsus est sed clārus nōn est.

_____

_____ **III. ANALYSIS EXERCISE** _____

> ### ANALYSIS QUESTION
>
> **We know that the accusative case shows us which nouns in a sentence are direct objects. What other uses does the accusative case have in Latin?**

Turn to the *Index Verbōrum* on page LXXXI and write the definition given for the word *prope* on the line below.

_____

When we say that an object is *near* or *next to* some other object, we are really talking about the *position* of that object—that is, where it is located in relation to other persons or objects.

It is appropriate, then, to note that words that tell us the *position* of persons or objects are called **prepositions.** *Prope* is a Latin preposition that we have just learned in this chapter. It will help us to find some other uses for the accusative case in Latin. Answer the questions below.

1. In the story about Quintus Caecilius Fēlix, we find the preposition *prope* used twice in caption 8. Carefully copy the *first* sentence that contains *prope* in the blank below, then answer the questions about it.

_____

2. What is the subject of the sentence?

_____

3. What is the verb?

_____

4. What is the *case* of the word for *wall?*

_____

5. Where is the Latin word for *wall* placed in relation to the preposition *prope?*

_____

6. Circle the word that is the direct object of the sentence (i.e., the one that receives the action of being placed).
   a) wall   **b)** vase

7. Translate the entire sentence in the space below.

_____

CONCLUSION No. 1

A noun that follows the preposition *prope* will *always* be in the accusative case even though it is not the direct object of the sentence.

---

8. Now go back to the story about Quintus and copy the *second* sentence of the seventh caption in the space below.

_____

NOTĀ BENE

The word *in* is another Latin preposition that describes location or position.

---

9. What is the subject of this new sentence you wrote above?

_____

10. What is the verb?

_____

11. Translate this verb into English.

_____

12. What is the *case* of the word for *garden*?

_____

13. Where is the Latin word for *garden* placed in relation to the preposition *in*?

_____

14. In the *Index Verbōrum* on page LXXXI, there are *two* definitions given for the Latin preposition *in*. Copy the preposition, the note in parentheses, and the English translation for the definition that applies in this particular instance.

_____

15. Write *yes* or *no* in the blanks to respond to these questions.

     a) _____ Is the word for *garden* the direct object of the sentence? (That is, is it the garden that gets *walked*?)
     b) _____ Is the word for *garden* the place (position) where the walking takes place?
     c) _____ Is there a direct object at all in this sentence?

16. Translate the entire sentence in the space below.

_____

> ## CONCLUSION No. 2
>
> A noun that follows the Latin preposition *in* will be in the accusative case when *in* has the meaning of *into*.
>
> This is true even though it is not the direct object of the sentence.

LET'S CHECK OUR TWO CONCLUSIONS

17. Go back to the eighth caption of the story and this time, copy the *last* sentence. Be sure you copy the entire sentence, then answer the questions about it.

_____

18. The same verb appears twice in this sentence. What is it?

_____

19. On the line below, list all of the words that are in the accusative case *in the order in which they appear in the sentence.*

_____

20. Only two of these words are direct objects. Which one is the direct object of the *first* verb? (That is, which word is receiving the action of being placed?)

_____

21. Which is the direct object of the *second* verb?

_____

22. Finally, can you explain, in your own words, why the other two words are also in the accusative case?

_____

_____

_____

_____

ANALYSIS ANSWER

In Latin, the accusative case is used for words that are direct objects, that is, for those words that directly receive the action of the verb.

In addition, nouns that immediately follow the preposition _____ *will always* be in the accusative case, even though they are not the direct objects of the sentence.

Nouns that immediately follow the Latin preposition _____ will also be in the accusative case when this preposition has the meaning of

_____ in English.

Look at the seventh caption once again from the story about Quintus Caecilius. Copy the first two sentences on the two lines below.

_____

_____

What is the subject of the second sentence?

_____

What is the accusative form of this name?

_____

NOTĀ BENE

We have learned that the nominative forms of first declension nouns usually end in the letter _____ , and that second declension nouns have nominative forms that usually end in the letters _____ or _____ .

Clēmens is a *third* declension noun. Nouns of this declension have a variety of nominative endings, and they form the accusative in a different way from first and second declension nouns. Notice, however, that *Clēmentem* (like all masculine and feminine nouns) still ends with the same letter that is characteristic of the accusative case (the letter m).

Clēmens, Clēmentem

DID YOU KNOW . . . ?

Roman women, especially those who were wealthy, were accustomed to spending time and money on beauty aids. Cosmetics of many varieties were available: chalk to whiten the skin, lipsticks, rouge and eye liners. Women spent hours preparing elaborate hairstyles for special occasions, dyed their hair, and were especially fond of blonde wigs. An orangish-red dye made from the henna plant was used to color fingernails, toenails and even the palms of the hands and the soles of the feet. Archaeologists have uncovered compacts, mirrors and vanity cases in the course of their excavations.

NŌMEN _____

DIĒS _____

_____ IV. EXERCITĀTIŌNĒS _____

A) Each of the sentences below contains the preposition *prope*. Complete each sentence with the proper Latin translation of the English word given, then translate your sentence into GOOD English. Be careful of the *case* of your noun.

1. (wall) Quintus prope _____ est.

   _____

2. (Mark) Aqua est in urnā prope _____ .

   _____

3. (door) Puer puellam prope _____ amat.

   _____

4. (student) Prope _____ formōsam grammaticus Graecus librum Graecum locat. (Careful on this one . . .)

   _____

   _____

5. (teacher) Marius puellam prope _____ nōn amat.

   _____

6. (kitchen) Puella formōsa et puer formōsus sunt prope _____ . Amīcī sunt.

   _____

   _____

B) Translate the following sentences into GOOD English. Be careful of the endings on the adjectives. They tell you which noun the adjective describes.

1. Agricola prope culīnam nōn est. Magnus et formōsus est.

   _____

   _____

2. Valeria hodiē cibum amat. Parāta est.

   _____

3. Poēta aquam portat. Clāra est.

   _____

4. Discipula capsārium monet. Laetus nōn est.

   _____

C) The next four sentences are similar to the first four sentences in this exercise, only this time you must translate from English to Latin. Remember, the gender of the adjective has to agree with the gender of the noun that it describes. Be sure to put the verb at the end of the sentence where it belongs.

1. Mark has a girlfriend. She is Greek.

   _____

2. The servant girl carries the vase. It is wet.

   _____

3. Julia sees a horse. It is beautiful.

   _____

4. Julius does not have a pen. He is angry.

   _____

D) Fill in the blanks with the appropriate Latin forms (ablative or accusative) of the words given in parentheses and watch the preposition *in* change meaning. Translate the entire sentence into GOOD English.

1. Servus in _____ est sed laetus hodiē nōn est.
   (KITCHEN)

   _____

2. Rānam in _____ Quintus nōn locat. Parva est.
   (BED)

   _____

3. Gallus in _____ iterum est et serva laeta nōn est.
   (ROAD)

   _____

4. Puella sellam parvam in _____ portat.
   (KITCHEN)

   _____

5. Paedagōgus prope fenestram in _____ poētam videt.
   (SCHOOL)

   _____

6. In _____ taurus magnus nōn ambulat.
   (WATER)

   Asinus in _____ ambulat.
   (GARDEN)

   _____

   _____

7. Vergilius in _____ ambulat sed servus in _____ nōn est.
   (KITCHEN)   (KITCHEN)

   _____

LECTIO VII

Reading, Writing, and Arithmetic: Roman Schools

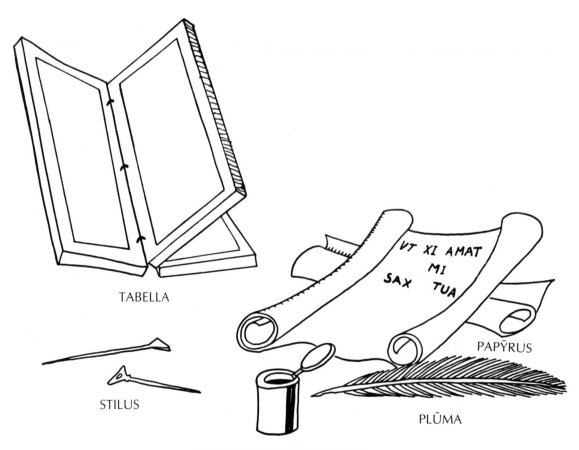

TABELLA

STILUS

ROMAN WRITING UTENSILS

VT XI AMAT
MI
SAX   TUA

PAPȲRUS

PLŪMA

NARRĀTIO

WHAT A SCHOOL IS . . .

Before you begin to read about Roman schools, take the time to write your own definition of the word *school* in the space that follows. Imagine, for example, that you had to explain to a person from another planet that you spend each of your weekdays in a place called *school*. How would you describe that place to this planetary visitor so that he or she could understand what a school is, what happens there and with whom you spend your time? Write a brief description of *school* in the space that follows or use a separate sheet of paper for a longer description.

A school is _____

_____

_____

_____

_____

_____

_____

Now look up the word *school* in a dictionary and in the space below, write down ALL of the definitions you find.

_____

_____

_____

_____

_____

_____

We usually aren't in the habit of looking up such common words as *school* in the dictionary because these are words that we use every day and we generally feel that we know what they mean. Were you surprised at any of the definitions you found? Were there more possibilities than you thought there would be? Compare your definitions with those of your classmates and write down any other definitions that you may not have included in your list.

GOING TO SCHOOL IN ANCIENT ROME

A *school*—for most Americans—means a building with many classrooms, a few offices, a library, and probably a gymnasium and a cafeteria. Schools are filled with students and teachers who spend a lot of time talking with each other and discussing all sorts of topics. They interact with each other in many different types of activities and generally learn from each other and from their discussions and activities. *School* is one of the institutions that our society uses to transfer our history, ideas, and values from one generation to the next.

That's not exactly what it was like to go to *school* in ancient Rome. Roman schools were quite different from our present-day concept of what a school is.

A Roman "school" usually consisted of approximately 20 to 30 students and one teacher. Students and teachers were almost always men. Only rarely were girls permitted to attend school. There were no desks, although sometimes there was a blackboard. In fact, classes were usually not even held in a building at all. It was much more customary for a teacher simply to gather his pupils about him under a tree or under the awning outside some shop.

Although Roman students did not have each weekend free as we do, regular classes were suspended every ninth day and, of course, at the times of the great religious festivals. Very often, schools would close during the summer months when the heat made holding classes uncomfortable. This was especially true in country schools, which released their students to help with the olive and grape harvests.

Since Roman schools were privately owned, parents had to pay tuition directly to the teacher for the privilege of sending their children to school to learn. In addition, a special slave called a ***paedagōgus*** usually accompanied his young master to and from school. Wealthy students might also have a ***capsārius*** to carry their books, and the very wealthy were often taught at home by private tutors.

Roman schools were often run by Greek freedmen teachers (the ***magister***) or sometimes by educated Greek slaves. Although the Roman legions conquered Greece and brought many Greeks back to Rome as slaves, the Romans greatly admired the culture and civilization of the Greek people. A man's education was not considered complete unless he had read the *Iliad* and the *Odyssey* by the Greek writer Homer, or had memorized whole passages from the works of other Greek writers like Sophocles and Euripides.

As for their writing utensils, students most often wrote with a ***stilus*** on a wooden tablet called a ***tabula*** or a ***tabella*** that was covered with a light coat of wax. A ***stilus*** was a stick that had a point on one end and was flattened on the other. The pointed end was used to carve letters into the waxed surface of the **tabella.** The flattened end of the **stilus** was used to smooth the wax when a mistake was made or to erase what was written on the **tabella** so that it could be used again. Sometimes, several **tabellae** were fastened together to make a sort of reuseable tablet.

A rough type of paper made from the papyrus reed was also available, but it was used less frequently because it was more expensive. Students wrote on papyrus with black ink made from soot and used a reed pen called a **calamus** or a quill pen called a **plūma.**

THE LŪDUS AND THE SCHOLA

The Romans had two words in Latin for school: **lūdus** and **schola.** The **lūdus** was roughly equivalent to our elementary school. Boys of the middle and professional classes attended the **lūdus** usually between the ages of 7 to 12. There were some girls in the **lūdī,** but as a general rule, girls were kept at home and trained by their mothers in household management, spinning, and weaving.

At the **lūdus,** children studied the basic subjects that were considered essential to becoming a well-rounded citizen: elementary arithmetic as well as reading and writing in both Latin and Greek. The principal method of teaching was simple repetition. Students listened while the **magister** (or the **litterātor,** as he was often called) read or recited from such Roman writers as Vergil, Ovid, and Juvenal, or from favorite Greek writers. To train the memory, they learned long passages of prose and poetry by heart in both Latin and Greek. There was little or no attempt to vary the pace or presentation of the material, and discipline in Roman schools was very strict. Quintus's caper with the frog would probably have earned him a severe flogging.

Many students finished their schooling with the **lūdus** at about 11 or 12 years of age. However, upon completing his work in the **lūdus,** a student might choose to continue studying in a Roman **schola.** The word **schola** comes from a Greek word that means *leisure.* Therefore, the **schola** was a school where studies were continued at the "leisure" of the student. Courses were taught by a **grammaticus** and were more specialized. They included Latin and Greek grammar, literature, geometry, astronomy, and music. Students read aloud and memorized passages from speeches by Cicero and the philosophic writings of Seneca.

The course of study in the **schola** was usually three or four years. Beyond that, a few students went on to study advanced literature and the art of public speaking from a **rhētor.** Public speaking was an extremely important art, especially for those who expected to enter public life and hold some government office. Besides, arguing and discussing topics of current interest were favorite pastimes of Roman men. The **rhētor** taught his students to argue convincingly, to vary the tone of their voices appropriately, and to use gestures to the best advantage.

Although the Romans were masters in construction methods and architecture, the study of the sciences and of technical subjects had no place in Roman schools. People whose jobs required a technical knowledge of some sort usually learned their trade on the job, as an apprentice. Schools were reserved for the basics of reading, writing, and arithmetic as well as the appreciation of fine literature and the ability to speak eloquently. Sometimes, however, there were specialized schools for training in music, the military, philosophy, and the sciences. There were even schools for training gladiators!

_____ **I. SELF-TEST** _____

Here is a quick way to test yourself to see how much you know about Roman schools. Write *True* or *False* in the space on the left.

_____ **1.** *Lūdus* and *schola* both mean *school* in Latin.

_____ **2.** The *lūdus* was roughly equivalent to our *high school*.

_____ **3.** Roman children began school at the age of 7.

_____ **4.** Roman schools usually consisted of one teacher and a few students.

_____ **5.** Roman girls were not allowed to attend schools and were educated at home.

_____ **6.** Education was free for all Roman citizens.

_____ **7.** Much emphasis was placed on repetition and memorization.

_____ **8.** Roman students wrote on wax-coated tablets. Pen and ink were unknown at the time of the Roman Empire.

_____ **9.** The *grammaticus* was a secondary school teacher.

_____ **10.** Courses in the *schola* were more specialized.

_____ **11.** Vergil was a famous Roman writer.

_____ **12.** Sophocles was another famous Roman writer.

_____ **13.** Greek and Roman writers as well as the Greek language were studied in secondary school.

_____ **14.** The Romans highly admired Greek culture and civilization and were greatly influenced by it.

_____ **15.** Most students completed work in the *lūdus* and the *schola*, then went on to study public speaking with a *rhētor*.

_____ **16.** For those students interested in learning a trade, science and technical subjects were taught in Roman schools in addition to courses in language and literature.

THE MEANING OF WORDS

You have probably heard it said that the Eskimos have dozens and dozens of words in their language that mean *snow*. Just as snow plays an influential and important role in the lives of a people who live in the far northern regions of the globe, the automobile is central to our lives in 20th-century America.

There are 28 words listed below. All of them represent some sort of vehicle used for transportation. This list is by no means complete. Can you think of any others?

bicycle	sedan	carriage	taxi
limousine	tractor	hot rod	cart
roadster	Rolls Royce	Cadillac	train
stagecoach	scooter	ricksha	tricycle
bus	convertible	trolley	chariot
touring car	truck	Honda	van
Model-T	buggy	station wagon	Plymouth

Even though all of these words mean essentially the same thing—vehicle—each of them is unique in the exact image it suggests. For example, if you came to school each day in a limousine, it would most probably indicate something about your personal situation that would be quite different than if you came to school each day on a tractor.

When we translate from one language to another, we sometimes have to take these "cultural" differences into consideration in order to portray an accurate picture of what is happening. At other times, it may not be important to make those distinctions. Consider the two sentences below. How does the second sentence affect your opinion of "grandma"?

EXAMPLE: My grandmother bought a car last week.
My grandmother bought a candy-apple red Jaguar convertible!

> ## NOTĀ BENE
>
> The language we speak is much more than just a collection of different kinds of words strung together to form sentences and ideas. In fact, you could memorize every word in the dictionary and still be unable to communicate intelligently with others. That's because language is not an isolated code and it does not exist independently from the culture in which it develops.
>
> We've said it before and we're going to say it once again:
>
> **When we translate our ideas and thoughts from one language to another, we must really be able to translate *meaning*, not only *words*.**

Now are you beginning to understand just how important that idea is in order to communicate with people from another culture?

___ II. TRANSLATING MEANING INSTEAD OF WORDS ___

The exercise below is a special translation exercise that concentrates on some of the new words we learned in this chapter for *school*, *pen*, *teacher*, and *slave*.

school	**lūdus, schola**
pen	**calamus, stilus, plūma**
teacher	**magister, grammaticus, rhētor**
slave	**capsārius, paedagōgus, servus, serva**

A) Translate these first six sentences from English into Latin. Choose the specific Latin word that conveys the exact meaning of the underlined portion of the sentence. Remember: *Translate meaning, not words.*

1. The <u>secondary school teacher</u> is a grammar school teacher, also.

    _____

2. Mandūcus is a <u>slave who takes care of the children at home.</u> Today, he is tired and angry.

    _____

3. Lucius is a little boy. He is in _school_ today.

_____

4. Caecilius is a big boy. He is in _school_ today, too.

_____

5. Antonio puts the _writing utensil_ next to the _waxed wooden tablet_.

_____

6. Clēmens has _a waxed tablet hooked together_.

_____

B) Now, using Part A as a model, translate the following sentences into GOOD English.

1. Gāius est _capsārius_. Graecus et prōcērus est.

_____

_____

2. Silvia _calamum_ prope papȳrum locat.

_____

3. _Magister_ in hortō prope _lūdum_ est.

_____

_____

4. Octāvius in _scholā_ est hodiē sed Marcus in _lūdō_ est.

_____

_____

5. _Grammaticus tabellam_ habet. Parva est _tabella_. Stilum prope _tabellam_ locat.

_____

_____

6. Minimē, _paedagōgus_ hodiē in scholā nōn est.

_____

_____

Study the new vocabulary in the *Index Verbōrum*, then read the *Mini-Fābula* about
Lūcrētius Tullius Frīvolus.

INDEX VERBŌRUM

fāma	fame, reputation	**quis?** who?	
habitat	(he, she, it) lives	**studiōsus, studiōsa**	eager, studious
lacus	lake	**stupidus, stupida**	stupid, dull
quaestio	(f.) question		

MINI-FĀBULA

Lūcrētius Tullius Frīvolus

1. Lūcrētius rāna Rōmāna est. Magna et
   formōsa est. Prope lacum lātum habitat.

2. Lūcrētius est discipulus. Lūcrētius
   quaestiōnem in scholā hodiē habet:
   "Quis est Gāius Iūlius Caesar?"

3. Magister īrātus est! Gāius Iūlius Caesar
   famōsus est! Caesar fāmam magnam habet. Quaestio stupida est. Rāna studiōsa
   nōn est. Discipulus stupidus est!

NOTĀ BENE

Look at the *fābula* and find the accusative form of the new noun, *quaestio*. Write

it here: _____ . We saw a similar accusative ending on
another word on page XCII. Write that word in these spaces:

_____ , _____ .
(NOMINATIVE)   (ACCUSATIVE)

Since *quaestio* does not end in *a* or *us*, it does not follow the same rules for the
accusative as the other nouns we have studied. *Quaestio* is a third declension
noun.

LECTIO VIII

The Latin Connection

Roman galleys such as these helped make the physical connection between Rome and the far reaches of the vast Roman Empire.

MAKING THE LATIN CONNECTION

DERIVATIVES: WORDS PASSED DOWN TO US FROM ANCIENT ROMAN TIMES

You have probably heard people say that a knowledge of Latin will help you understand English better. One of the main reasons why that statement is true is that more than 65 percent of all the words used in English come to us either directly or indirectly from Latin.

Did you know that? Well, it's true. And that's only ONE of the reasons why Latin will help us to understand our own language. There are others, too, but before we go into them, let's take a look at some of these words that we've borrowed from our Roman ancestors.

MANUS (HAND)
MANICURE

Do you recognize any of the Latin words in the list below? Two thousand years ago, the Romans were using these very words every day with exactly the same spelling and meaning as their present-day English counterparts. They haven't changed at all from their original Latin forms.

jūnior	major
senior	minor
plūs	maximum
minus	minimum
arēna	spectātor
audītōrium	formula

On their long journey through the centuries, however, some of the Latin words that we've borrowed did change a little here and there. The result is that our modern forms of these original Latin words are slightly different but still recognizable. Look at the similarity of these English words to their Latin ancestors.

LATIN	ENGLISH
centum	cent
flamma	flame
liquidus	liquid
persōna	person
rārus	rare
soccus	sock (for the foot)
taedium	tedium
vēna	vein

NŌMEN _____

DIĒS _____

Here is a list of 10 common English words. Find the Latin word in the second column that was the ancient cousin to our modern-day English word. Draw a line between the two related words to *make the Latin connection.*

ENGLISH

1. antique
2. dignity
3. annual
4. famous
5. elegance
6. gravity
7. imbecile
8. ignition
9. populate
10. pork

LATIN

1. ignis (fire)
2. fāmōsus (much spoken of)
3. dignus (worthy)
4. gravis (heavy, weighty)
5. antīquus (ancient)
6. imbēcillus (weak, feeble)
7. populus (a people, a nation)
8. annus (year)
9. porcus (pig, hog)
10. ēlegans (fine, tasteful)

Derivatives All Around Us: How to Recognize Them

The relationship between the English word *antique* and the Latin word *antīquus* is pretty obvious, and besides, there's a good chance that you have already met up with the word *antique* before.

But stop and think about it for a minute. If more than 65 percent of all English words are based on Latin, that means that the same method that we used in the exercise above to *make the Latin connection* can be used to figure out the meanings of lots of other English words, too. In fact, you'll be surprised at how often words that you think you don't know become perfectly understandable and transparent when you look at them as possible Latin derivatives. Even the little bit of Latin that you have learned so far will help you to see all sorts of clues. Those clues will help you figure out the meanings of literally thousands of words.

When you finish this book, you will have learned more than 200 Latin vocabulary words. That's really not very many, especially when you consider that to be among the top 10 percent of adult speakers of English, you need to know at least 80,000 words! Many of the Latin words that you are learning, however, have survived the trip through time and have come into English in several different forms.

Take, for example, the Latin word *ignis*, which means *fire*. This one Latin root word has given us at least three English words. They all have similar meanings—each having something to do with the idea of *fire*, naturally.

Ignis is the *Latin root word* for:

ignition
ignite
igneous

The English word IGNITION is from the Latin root word for "fire," IGNIS.

NŌMEN_____

DIĒS_____

Notice that each of these three English words contains the original *Latin root word* (**igni** or **igne**) in some form. You are probably familiar with the first two words.

- You probably already know that the **ignition** of an automobile is the mechanism that is responsible for *firing up* the engine.
- And you already know that when the directions on a can of charcoal starter say: "Use caution when **igniting** the charcoal," that it really means: "Use caution when you *set fire to* the charcoal."
- But what about that third word, **igneous?** You may or may not know what **igneous** means. Of course, since you are studying Latin and you already know that *ignis* means *fire*, you've probably already guessed that **igneous** must have something to do with fire, and you're right. Read on.

Suppose that you are assigned a chapter to read in your science class and you . . . well . . . never quite get around to reading it. Then suppose that the next morning when you go to class, the teacher passes out a quiz on the chapter. Not good!

Luckily, however, you've been studying Latin. Here is one of the questions from that quiz. Using what you know from your Latin class, how would you answer it?

Which of the following is an **igneous** rock? Circle the correct answer.

      a) granite
      b) sandstone
      c) lava
      d) quartz

Did you choose *c* as the correct response? Whether you did or didn't, explain below in your own words why *c* is the correct answer.

_____

See what we mean about Latin helping us with English and—who ever would have thought—science, too. Of course, this is only one example, but there is one thing that we can pretty much promise you. Once you have finished this chapter, you're going to be seeing Latin derivative words all over the place! And because of that, you'll probably even surprise yourself with how many times you'll be able to guess the meaning of a word correctly just because you know some Latin.

Before we begin the exercise on the next page, it might be a good idea to review ALL of the vocabulary words that we have learned so far in this book. Turn to each page listed below. When you feel that you know the vocabulary listed on that page, make a check in the box next to the page number and go on to the next page listed. When you have checked all of the boxes, you are ready to do Exercise 1.

☐ page XXIII   ☐ page XXXIV   ☐ page CII
☐ page XXXI   ☐ page XLIX   ☐ page CIV
☐ pages XXXII–XXXIII ☐ page LXXXI

MAKE THE LATIN CONNECTIONS

I. EXERCITĀTIŌNĒS

MAKE THE LATIN CONNECTION

A) Follow the directions below carefully. Use the vocabularies listed above and rely on your own knowledge of Latin to find the answers. DO NOT USE A DICTIONARY.

Directions for the Exercise

1. Each problem in this exercise contains five blanks marked *a, b, c, d,* and *e.* Look at the italicized word in each sentence and decide from which Latin word it comes. Choose your answer from the list given at the top of the page. Write the Latin root word in blank *a.*
2. In blank *b,* write the English translation of the Latin word you have chosen.
3. Now read the entire sentence and, using what you know about the Latin root word, complete blank *c* with the logical response.

> Caution: Make sure that your final sentence reads
> as a correct English sentence.

4. Finally, complete blanks *d* and *e* to *make the Latin connection.*
5. To check your work, compare answers *d* and *e.* They should be words that look pretty much alike. Otherwise, there would be no *Latin connection,* would there?

EXAMPLE: **a)** ____contentus____

b) ____happy____

c) A ____contented____ cow is a ____happy____ cow.

d) The English word ____contented____ comes from the

e) Latin word ____contentus____ .

CHECK: *Contented* and *contentus* resemble each other. Therefore, the answer is probably right.

THE LIST

agricola	fenestra	cathēdra	mūrus
equus	lūna	albus	amīcus
bonus	discipulus		

1. **a)** _____

   b) _____

   c) A *mural* is a painting on a _____ .

   d) The English word _____ comes from the

   e) Latin word _____ .

2. **a)** _____

   b) _____

   c) One lands a *lunar* module on the _____ .

   d) The English word _____ comes from the

   e) Latin word _____ .

3. **a)** _____

   b) _____

   c) An *equestrian* demonstration is a demonstration of

   _____ .

   d) The English word _____ comes from the

   e) Latin word _____ .

4. **a)** ————————

   b) ————————

   c) A *fenestrated* wall contains many ——————— .

   d) The English word ——————— comes from the

   e) Latin word ——————— .

5. **a)** ————————

   b) ————————

   c) The *albumen* of an egg is the part that is ———————
   when it is cooked.

   d) The English word ——————— comes from the

   e) Latin word ——————— .

6. **a)** ————————

   b) ————————

   c) A *disciple* of Freud is a ——————— or follower of Freud.

   d) The English word ——————— comes from the

   e) Latin word ——————— .

7. **a)** ————————

   b) ————————

   c) *Agriculture* is something with which ——————— need to be
   concerned.

   d) The English word ——————— comes from the

   e) Latin word ——————— .

8. **a)** ————————

   b) ————————

   c) Employees get Christmas *bonuses* for doing a ——————— job.

   d) The English word ——————— comes from the

   e) Latin word ——————— .

9. a) _____

   b) _____

    c) Someone with an *amicable* disposition is a _____ ly person.

   d) The English word _____ comes from the

   e) Latin word _____ .

USE YOUR HEAD ON THIS ONE FOR TWO EXTRA POINTS!

10. a) _____

    b) _____

    c) A *cathedral* is the _____ of religion.

    d) The English word _____ comes from the

    e) Latin word _____ .

B) Each italicized word in the sentences below is a good English word. You may not know the meaning of all of them, but do not use a dictionary to do this exercise. See if you can use what you know about Latin to figure out what each word means. Complete this exercise by following the directions for Part A.

THE LIST

fīdus	quattuor
malus	*novus*
asinus	*lātus*
albus	*īrātus*

1. a) _____

   b) _____

    c) Panthers are big, black cats, but a panther afflicted with *albinism* is probably _____ in color.

   d) The English word _____ comes from the

   e) Latin word _____ .

2. a) _____

    b) _____

        c) Bob divorced Marge on grounds of *infidelity*, which probably means that

        she was not _____ to him.

    d) The English word _____ comes from the

    e) Latin word _____ .

3. a) _____

    b) _____

        c) A *malicious* act is one that is intentionally _____ .

    d) The English word _____ comes from the

    e) Latin word _____ .

4. a) _____

    b) _____

        c) Since they said he was a *novice* monk, I suspect that he was

        _____ to the order.

    d) The English word _____ comes from the

    e) Latin word _____ .

FĀTĪGATUS (TIRED)
FATIGUE

5. a) _____

   b) _____

       c) **If I told you that Joe has an *irascible* personality, you would know that**

         he is _____ a lot of the time.

   d) The English word _____ comes from the

   e) Latin word _____ .

BE CAREFUL ABOUT THIS LAST ONE!

6. a) _____   _____

   b) _____   _____

       c) **A *quadrilateral* enclosure is a place with _____ _____ .**

   d) The English word _____ comes from the TWO Latin

   e) words _____ and _____ .

C) Now try these on your own. Write the Latin root word from which each of the following English words is derived.

   1. library   _____   **4.** magnify   _____

   2. optimist   _____   **5.** longevity   _____

   3. aquarium   _____   **6.** horticulture_____

D) Can you explain in your own words what each of the examples in Exercise C "means" in terms of its Latin root, just as you did in Exercises A and B? When you have finished, draw an arrow from the Latin root to its English derivative. Here's an example:

       Mūrus = wall: A *mural* is a painting on a *wall.*

1. _____

    _____

2. _____

    _____

3. _____

_____

4. _____

_____

5. _____

_____

6. _____

_____

E) Make the Latin Connection between these two lists of common English and Latin words by drawing a line between the two words that are related. Be careful. There are more words in the Latin list than you need and some of them may be used more than once.

ENGLISH	LATIN
1. nominate	1. tabula
2. pronoun	2. parātus
3. tabulate	3. via
4. lunatic	4. nōmen
5. viaduct	5. servus
6. service	6. septem
	7. lūna

F) There are four common Latin words below. Write the English translation of each in the blank next to the word, then see how many English derivative words you can list that are based on the original Latin. Compare your answers with your classmates' and add new words to your list that you might have overlooked. Answers will vary.

1. *Schola:* _____   3. *Magnus:* _____

2. *Aqua:* _____   4. *Quattuor:* _____

LECTIO IX

The Interrogative and the Negative:
Why Not a Little Variety?

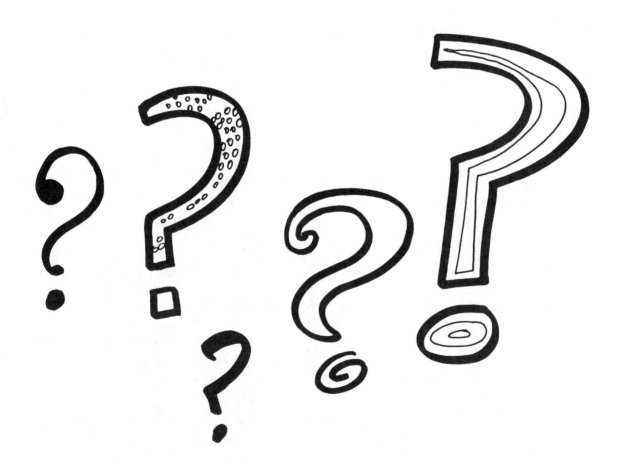

_____ I. ANALYSIS EXERCISE _____

> ### ANALYSIS QUESTION
>
> **How do we ask a question in Latin?**

HOW WE ASK A QUESTION IN ENGLISH

Before we can answer the Analysis Question about Latin, it is probably a good idea to take a look at our own English language to see how we ask questions in English.

Look at the four example sentences below. The two sentences on the left are *declarative sentences,* that is, they make a *simple declaration or statement of fact.*

The two sentences on the right are ***interrogative sentences.*** Interrogative sentences *ask a question.*

DECLARATIVE SENTENCES	INTERROGATIVE SENTENCES
1. Paul sees a horse.	1. Does Paul see a horse?
2. The boy has a horse.	2. Does the boy have a horse?

Declarative sentences and interrogative sentences are not new to you, even though you may never have called them by these names. You've been asking questions ever since you were a tiny child, and even today you couldn't make it through a whole day without using both declarative and interrogative sentences.

So if you already know all about how to ask questions, what's the big deal, you may wonder?

Although we can all ask questions correctly, we aren't always aware of just exactly how we change the structure of a sentence to make it into a question. By taking a look at what we do in English (what we already know) we will understand more easily how questions are formed in Latin (what we don't know yet and are about to learn).

Answer the questions in the following exercise based on the four example sentences you just read.

1. Look at the first declarative sentence and answer the following questions based on it.
   a) What is the subject of the sentence?

_____

b) What is the verb of the sentence?

_____

c) What is the direct object of the sentence?

_____

d) In the blanks below, write the words *subject, verb, object* in the order that these parts of speech appear in the first declarative sentence. The first blank has already been filled in.

_____subject_____, _____, _____

2. Copy the first interrogative sentence below.

_____

a) What is the subject of this sentence?

_____

b) What is the direct object of the sentence?

_____

c) Now be careful! Something has happened to the verb in this sentence. It is no longer only ONE word, but has become TWO words, a helping (or *auxiliary*) verb plus the main verb. Copy both of them in the spaces below.

_____, _____
(HELPING VERB)   (MAIN VERB)

d) Write the words *subject, helping verb, main verb, direct object* in the order that they appear in the first interrogative sentence.

_____ _____ _____ _____

NOTĀ BENE

When there are TWO words (a helping verb and a main verb) that are used together in this way, we call them a *verb form*. Here are some other *verb forms*:

He is walking.
We do go to class every day.
They are sleeping.
She has already bought it.
Have I seen him lately?

---

3. Now, read the following conclusion and make it a correct statement by writing the correct answers in the blanks. Use the knowledge that you've gained through doing this Analysis Exercise to guide you.

CONCLUSION NO. 1

One way to form a question from a declarative sentence *in English* is to add

the helping verb _____ to the main verb and to put this

helping verb _____ of the question. The
(AT THE BEGINNING/IN THE MIDDLE/AT THE END)

original verb then comes _____ the subject.
(BEFORE/AFTER)

***Does** Paul **see** the horse?*

HOW WE ASK A QUESTION IN LATIN

Now look at the Latin translations of our four original example sentences on page CXVIII. Answer the questions based on these sentences to find out what changes are needed in Latin to transform a declarative sentence into an interrogative sentence.

DECLARATIVE SENTENCES	INTERROGATIVE SENTENCES
1. Paulus equum videt.	1. Videtne Paulus equum? Videtne equum Paulus?
2. Puer equum habet.	2. Habetne puer equum? Habetne equum puer?

1. Where is the verb placed in each of the declarative sentences?

_____

Is this the "normal" place for a verb in Latin?

_____

2. Where is the verb placed in each of the interrogative sentences?

_____

3. Is there a set order for the subject and direct object in an interrogative sentence or can their positions be interchanged?

_____

4. What two-letter suffix is added to the first word of each interrogative sentence?

_____

CONCLUSION NO. 2

1. **In written English,** to indicate a question, we put a question mark at the end of a sentence. The question mark acts as a sign that tells us: "The sentence that preceded this mark was a question."
2. **In written Latin,** to indicate a question, we attach the suffix -ne to the end of the first word of the sentence. The Latin suffix -ne acts as a sign that tells us: "The sentence that begins with this word is going to be a question."
3. **The Latin suffix -ne is the exact equivalent of our question mark.** The only major difference, of course, is that the Romans put their -ne at the *beginning* of their sentences and we put our ? at the end of ours.
4. To conform to modern usage, when we write Latin sentences, we normally add the suffix -ne to the first word and also the question mark at the end of the sentence.
5. Although the first word of a question is usually the verb, exceptions to this rule are not uncommon:

(Does Paul have a horse?)

Paulusne equum habet?
(Does Paul have a horse?)

CAUTION! CAREFUL! WATCH OUT! WARNING!

(If you're getting the feeling that we're trying to say something important here, you're right! Turn the page and read the text in the box.)

NOTĀ BENE

Be careful not to make the mistake of equating the Latin suffix **-ne** with the English verb "does".

The suffix -ne is not—we repeat, IS NOT—the equivalent of *does*, and the word *does* is not used in translating every question beginning with -ne. Note the following sentence, for example:

Estne Quintus puer Rōmānus?
Is Quintus a Roman boy?

Latin has no word for our English word *DOES* when it is used as a helping verb in this way.

Therefore, when translating from English to Latin, we cannot translate *does* because there is no word in Latin that corresponds to our English word.

CONCLUSION No. 3

Now we are ready to draw a final conclusion about how questions are formed in Latin. Fill in the blanks to complete the rule correctly.

In Latin, to make a question out of a declarative sentence, we add the suffix

_____ to the end of the _____ word in the sentence. As a concession to modern usage, we also add a question mark to the end of the sentence even though the Romans did not use question marks. Very often, the first word of a question is the verb.

PLEASE NOTE:

The answer to a question formed
in this way will always be YES or NO.

QUESTION	ANSWER
Videtne puer puellam?	Ita vērō, puer puellam videt.
Does the boy see the girl?	Yes! The boy sees the girl.
	Minimē, puer puellam nōn videt.
	No, the boy does not see the girl.

NŌMEN _____

DIĒS _____

II. EXERCITĀTIŌNĒS

A) Change the following declarative statements into interrogative statements. Then translate the Latin question into English. In this exercise, make sure to put the verb FIRST in the sentence.

EXAMPLE: Līvius crētam prope papȳrum locat.

_____ Locatne Līvius crētam prope papȳrum? _____

_____ Does Livius put the chalk next to the paper? _____

1. Tēlemachus est grammaticus honestus et iustus.

   _____

   _____

2. Puella formōsa urnam prope casam magnam locat.

   _____

   _____

3. In lūdō iterum est discipulus studiōsus.

   _____

   _____

4. Equus albus in terrā ūmidā prope lacum ambulat.

   _____

   _____

5. Tiberius puellam Graecam et clāram monet.

   _____

   _____

6. Quintia quaestiōnem bonam habet.

   _____

   _____

7. Octāvius hodiē stultus est.

_____

_____

8. Serva nova asinum malum pulsat.

_____

_____

B) Underline the verbs in the sentences below. Be careful. Some of the sentences have a **verb form** composed of two words (that is, a helping verb plus the main verb). Translate each English question into Latin. Remember, even when there is a verb form composed of two verbs in English, Latin only has one. Make sure the direct object is in the accusative case.

1. Is Quintus tired today?

_____

2. Does the girl have a big horse?

_____

3. Does Julie love Julius?

_____

4. Is the Greek in the kitchen?

_____

5. Does the vase have water (in it)?

_____

6. Does the little girl hold the pen?

_____

7. Is the food good?

_____

8. Does the teacher hold the chalk?

_____

NŌMEN _____

DIĒS _____

_____ III. ANALYSIS EXERCISE _____

A) Study the five example sentences below. Read each question aloud, first in Latin (with its Latin answer), then in English (with its English answer).

EXAMPLES:			
a)	Estne Rufus Rōmānus? Ita, est.	**a)**	Is Rufus Roman? Yes (he is).
b)	Claudiane Rufum amat? Minimē, nōn amat.	**b)**	Does Claudia love Rufus? No (she doesn't).
c)	Quis est Tēlemachus? Tēlemachus est puer Graecus.	**c)**	Who is Telemachus? Telemachus is a Greek boy.
d)	Quid habet Tēlemachus? Tēlemachus librum habet.	**d)**	What does Telemachus have? Telemachus has a book.
e)	Ubi est liber? Liber prope cathēdram est.	**e)**	Where is the book? The book is next to the chair.

1. Notice that questions *a* and *b* must be answered "yes" or "no." Can we answer questions *c*, *d*, and *e* with "yes" or "no"?

   _____

2. Notice that questions *a* and *b* carry the suffix -ne on the first word. Do sentences *c*, *d*, and *e* carry the -ne suffix on the first word?

   _____

3. In the three blanks below, write the first words of Latin sentences *c*, *d*, and *e*.

   c) _____ **d)** _____ **e)** _____

> ### NOTĀ BENE
>
> These three words (in c, d, and e that you just filled in) are called **interrogative words.** Interrogative words are words that ask a question.
>
> These words do not need the suffix -ne because their meaning is already interrogative.

4. Write the first word of Latin sentences *a* and *b* in the blanks below.

a) _____   **b)** _____

Now write these words without the question suffix.

a) _____   **b)** _____

Are these words (without the suffix) *interrogative words?* Do they ALWAYS ask a question like *Ubi? Quis? Quid?* or are they sometimes used in ordinary, declarative sentences?

_____

CAN these words be interrogative words?

_____

What do we have to do to them to MAKE them interrogative?

_____

> ### CONCLUSION
>
> Not all Latin questions have the suffix -ne attached to the _____ word of the sentence. Some Latin questions begin with interrogative words such as
>
> _____? and _____? and _____?. These words do not require the suffix _____ because they are already interrogative.

THE ROMAN BATHS: A PLACE TO SEE AND BE SEEN

Nearly all Romans spent part of their afternoon at one of the many public bathing establishments called *balnea* or *thermae*. The baths served as a meeting place where people could go to relax, to discuss the events of the day with friends, and to be seen by others. In addition, personal hygiene and care of the body were regarded as highly esteemed pastimes by the Romans.

Since the *thermae* were very popular, they were sometimes extremely elaborate. For example, the baths at Caracalla could accommodate 1,600 bathers at one time. Hot air heated by furnaces and circulated under the floors kept both the water and the bathers warm and comfortable. Slaves were available to give massages and to rub the body with oils and perfumes. Since bathers customarily wore no clothing at the baths, there were separate facilities for men and women. The baths of Caracalla also included athletic facilities, gardens, and even libraries for the complete indulgence of its bathers.

B) Translate the word in parentheses to complete each question below. Then translate the whole sentence into GOOD English. Be sure to write both sentences out completely.

EXAMPLE: (Who) est Tēlemachus?

_____Quis est Tēlemachus?_____

_____Who is Telemachus?_____

1. (Where) est puer Rōmānus?

   _____

   _____

2. (What) tenet puella Graeca?

   _____

   _____

3. (Where) est capsārius?

   _____

   _____

4. (Who) portat urnam?

   _____

   _____

5. (What) habet Marcus in urnā?

   _____

   _____

6. (Who) pulsat puellam parvam?

   _____

   _____

7. (Where) puer rānam locat?

_____

_____

8. (Who) discipulam studiōsam videt?

_____

_____

C) Re-read the *Fābula* about *Quintus Cae-cilius Fēlix* in chapter VI. Then answer the following questions based on the story. Be sure to write your answer in Latin and use complete sentences.

1. Estne Quintus puer Rōmānus?

_____

2. Estne Quintus parvus?

_____

3. Estne Trānio paedagōgus?

_____

4. Estne Clēmens etiam paedagōgus?

_____

5. Quis est Theodorus?

_____

6. Ubi sunt hodiē Theodorus et Quintus?

_____

7. Quid videt Quintus?

_____

8. Quid portat Clēmens?

_____

9. Locatne Clēmens urnam prope mūrum?

_____

10. Ubi est rāna?

_____

11. Ubi locat urnam Quintus?

_____

12. Quis est īrātus?

_____

13. Quis est contentus?

_____

_____ IV. ANALYSIS EXERCISE _____

ANALYSIS QUESTION

How do we make a sentence negative in Latin?

AFFIRMATIVE OR NEGATIVE? . . .YES OR NO?

When somebody asks us a question, we can usually answer it in one of two ways. We can answer *affirmatively*, that is, with a *yes* answer, or we can answer *negatively*, that is, with a *no* answer.

Take a look at the affirmative and negative examples below.

AFFIRMATIVE

1. Mark *likes* the girl.
2. Mark *is* a Roman boy.

NEGATIVE

1. Mark *does not like* the girl.
2. Mark *is not* a Roman boy.

NOTĀ BENE

IN ENGLISH, the word that makes a sentence negative is the word *not*. It is usually placed *after the verb* when the verb is a single word. See example sentence 2 above.

When the verb is a verb form (i.e., composed of two or more words), *not* is usually placed *after the first (or helping) verb*. See the first example above.

Now look at these same two sentences translated into Latin.

AFFIRMATIVE

1. Marcus puellam amat.
2. Marcus est puer Rōmānus.

NEGATIVE

1. Marcus puellam nōn amat.
2. Marcus nōn est puer Rōmānus.

Based on your observations, fill in the following blanks to complete the conclusion about negative and affirmative sentences in Latin.

CONCLUSION

1. The Latin word which corresponds to our English word *not* is _____.

2. This Latin negative word is usually placed _____ the verb.
   (BEFORE/AFTER)

3. The position of the negative word in Latin is _____
   the position of the negative word in English.   (THE SAME AS/DIFFERENT FROM)

MORE ON NEGATIVE AND AFFIRMATIVE—THE LONG AND SHORT OF IT

1. Turn to page LXXXI and in the spaces below, copy the note on that page that explains how we use short affirmative and negative responses. Do not copy the example, please.

   _____

   _____

   _____

2. Now check the *Index Verbōrum* in the back of the book to find the EXACT English translation of these two Latin words:

   ita: _____

   minimē: _____

3. *In English*, when somebody asks us a "yes" or "no" question, we can usually answer in one of three ways:
   a) We can answer simply "yes" or "no," period.
   b) We can answer "yes" or "no" plus a partial statement.
   c) Or we can answer "yes" or "no" plus a full statement.

Look at these examples:

Does the girl like Mark?		**Amatne puella Marcum?**	
a)	Yes.	**a)**	_____
	No.		_____
b)	Yes, she does.	**b)**	Ita, amat.
	No, she doesn't.		Minimē, nōn amat.
c)	Yes, the girl likes Mark.	**c)**	Ita, puella Marcum amat.
	No, the girl does not like Mark.		Minimē, puella Marcum nōn amat.

4. Using what you have learned so far in this Analysis Exercise, write a statement in the space below explaining why there are blank lines opposite "yes" and "no" in the sentences labeled *a* above.

_____

_____

5. Using the *exact* definitions of *ita* and *minimē*, give the "literal" translation of the two Latin sentences below.

   A **"literal"** translation is an ***exact*** translation of the words from one language to another. It is often not a very good translation because it does not always translate the **meaning** of the sentence. **(A "good" translation translates *meaning* and not just *words*.)**

Latin		**English Equivalent**
Ita	=	_____
amat	=	_____

Now put them together for the "literal" translation.

Ita, amat	=	_____

Latin		**English Equivalent**
Minimē	=	_____
nōn amat	=	_____

Now put these together for the "literal" translation.

Minimē, nōn amat	=	_____

6. What is a "good" translation of the two sentences above?

_____

_____

CONCLUSION

To make a sentence negative in Latin, we place the word _____
immediately BEFORE the verb of the sentence.

Since Latin has no direct equivalent of our English words yes and *no*, in order

to answer affirmatively, a speaker of Latin usually used the word _____

and repeated the _____.

To answer negatively, a speaker of Latin used the word _____

and repeated the verb with the negative word _____ in
front of it.

V. EXERCITĀTIŌNĒS

A) Change the affirmative statements in this exercise to negative statements, then translate your answers into GOOD English. Watch the negative word change positions from Latin to English. Be careful! Some sentences may have more than one verb.

1. Agricola equum album habet.

_____

_____

2. Paulina in culīnā hodiē est.

_____

_____

3. Asinum fatīgātum servus fīdus pulsat.

   _____

   _____

4. Octāvius est grammaticus Graecus et in scholā hodiē est.

   _____

   _____

   _____

   _____

5. Habet magister stilum parvum.

   _____

   _____

6. Discipulus prope chartam crētam locat.

   _____

   _____

7. Puella urnam tenet et laeta est.

   _____

   _____

8. Quintus videt tabulam Latīnam.

   _____

   _____

9. Caecilius puellam prōcēram et formōsam videt.

   _____

   _____

10. Servus Rōmānus magistrum monet.

    _____

    _____

ROMAN DRESS: TOGAS, STOLAS, AND TROUSERS

The characteristic attire of the well-dressed Roman was a long, white, flowing garment called a *toga*. Although trousers existed in Roman times, they were most commonly worn by the barbaric tribes to the north. No self-respecting Roman would think of wearing such crude, inelegant clothing.

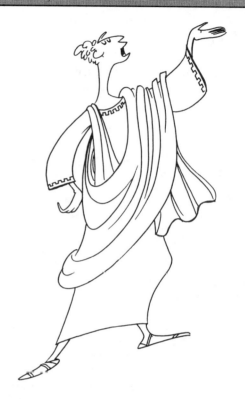

The toga was made of a large, single piece of cloth—usually wool—that was draped over the body in such a way that the left arm was covered, leaving the right arm free. It was worn over a loose-fitting, shirt-like garment called the *tunica* which fell nearly to the knees and was often belted. Slaves and common people usually wore only tunics when going about their daily tasks, but ALL Romans, regardless of rank, wore the white toga at public games, at court sessions, and on special festival days. The toga was a symbol of equality and citizenship.

Roman women also wore a tunica beneath a garment called a *stola* that was similar to the men's toga. The stola was draped elegantly over the body and reached to the ankles. Often, a woman would wear a decorative shawl called a *palla* over the stola. Of course, in the United States today, modern women still wear dresses but trousers have replaced the elegant, flowing toga as common dress for men. Nevertheless, the Roman toga as a symbol of achievement and equality is still evident in our modern society in the flowing robes of judges and the graduation gowns of school graduates.

B) Answer the following questions with a complete sentence in Latin. Do not use a partial statement here. Translate your answer into GOOD English. Answer according to the indications given.

EXAMPLE: Estne Quintus puella?

(No) _____Minimē, Quintus nŏn est puella._____

_____No, Quintus is not a girl._____

1. Estne Tēlemachus grammaticus Graecus?

(Yes) _____

_____

2. Habetne puella calamum bonum?

(No) _____

_____

3. Pulsatne Trānio Quintum et Matellam?

(Yes) _____

_____

4. Estne puer formōsus et honestus?

(Yes) _____

_____

5. Amatne Clāra Gāium?

(No) _____

_____

6. Tenetne Flāviam puer Rōmānus?

(No) _____

_____

C) Answer the following questions with a *partial statement*. Do not repeat the whole sentence. Then translate your answer into GOOD English. Read the example before you begin.

EXAMPLE: Amatne Publius grammaticum Rōmānum?

(No) _____Minimē, nōn amat._____

_____No, he doesn't._____

1. Estne Aurelia puella parva?

   (No) _____

   _____

2. Habetne poēta plūmam?

   (Yes) _____

   _____

3. Tenetne discipula papȳrum bonum?

   (No) _____

   _____

4. Portatne hodiē servus librum?

   (No) _____

   _____

5. Estne magna fenestra prope portam?

   (Yes) _____

   _____

6. Amatne Quintum et Portiam Lūcius?

   (Yes) _____

   _____

D) Translate the following questions and answers into Latin, paying special attention to the form of the yes/no answers. Check the Conclusion on page CXXXII to refresh your memory before you begin.

1. Does the teacher have the paper? Yes, he does.

   _____

2. Is the girl tall? Yes.

   _____

3. Does the farmer see the bull in the garden? No, he doesn't.

   _____

4. Does Marcia hold the little frog? Yes, she does.

   _____

5. Is the kitchen next to the garden? No.

   _____

6. Does the student carry the writing tablet and the paper? Yes.

   _____

   _____

E) Write three Latin questions that require a yes/no answer in the first blank space of each number below. Each of your questions must have at least six or seven words in it. Be sure to use only the vocabulary that you already know.

1. _____

_____

2. _____

_____

3. _____

_____

4. _____

_____

F) Write three Latin questions that begin with an interrogative word in the first blank space of each number below. Each of your questions must have at least six or seven words in it. Be sure to use only the vocabulary that you already know.

1. _____

_____

2. _____

_____

3. _____

_____

4. _____

_____

G) Go back to Exercises E and F. On the *second* line, write the answer (in Latin, of course) to each of the original questions you wrote.

LECTIO X

Fābula

MARCELLA ET ATTICUS BARBARUS

Marcella est puella Rōmāna. In vīllā magnā prope ōceanum habitat. Marcella discipula in scholā nōn est sed in vīllā. Estne contenta Marcella? Ita est et semper occupāta est.

Māterfamiliās est Lāvīnia. Fēmina honesta et iūcunda est sed Rōmāna nōn est. Lāvīnia est Hispāna. Vīllam magnam et familiam contentam habet Lāvīnia. Fīliam Marcellam amat.

Lāvīnia in hortō prope ōceanum hodiē est. Serva fīda et Marcella in hortō etiam sunt. Lāvīnia virum prope vīllam videt. Quis est vir? Estne paterfamiliās? Minimē, nōn est. Vergilius in vīllā hodiē nōn est. Estne amīcus aut vir inimīcus? Quis est?

Nunc vir prope Lāvīniam est. Est Trebius, amīcus bonus. Lāvīnia laeta est. Marcella Trebium amat. Semper fābulam bonam narrat. Quid est fābula hodiē? Atticus Barbarus! Marcella auscultat. . . .

Atticus est barbarus et captīvus Rōmānus. Estne etiam gladiātor? Ita est et in harēnā publicā saepe pugnat. Gladiātor fāmōsus est. Magnus et validus etiam est sed formōsus nōn est.

Atticus in harēnā hodiē est. Gladium longum portat. Taurus ferus in harēnā etiam est. Atticus taurum nōn amat. Taurus Atticum vulnerat. Estne timidus Atticus? Minimē, nōn est. Gladiātor semper est validus. Taurum pulsat.

Atticus est contentus. Populī Rōmānī sunt contentī! Victōria est magna!

Marcella etiam contenta est! Fābula optima est! Sed tempus fugit. Fābulam terminat. Amīcus Trebius est narrātor bonus.

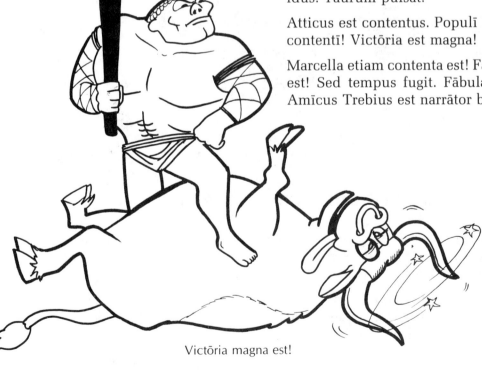

Victōria magna est!

INDEX VERBŌRUM

NOUNS

captīvus   prisoner
fēmina   woman
fīlia   daughter
fīlius   son
gladiātor   (m.) gladiator (one hired to fight at public shows)
gladius   sword
harēna   sand (by extension: the arena of the amphitheater, which was covered with sand)

māterfamiliās   mother of the family, female head of the family
narrātor   (m.) narrator, storyteller
ōceanus   ocean
paterfamiliās   father of the family, male head of the family
victōria   victory
vīlla   country house, estate
vir, virum   man

ADJECTIVES

barbarus, barbara   foreign, uncultivated, strange
fāmōsus, fāmōsa   famous
ferus, fera   wild, untamed
formōsus, formōsa   beautiful, handsome
Hispānus, Hispāna   Spanish
inimīcus, inimīca   unfriendly

iūcundus, iūcunda   pleasant, agreeable
occupātus, occupāta   busy, occupied
publicus, publica   public
studiōsus, studiōsa   eager, studious
timidus, timida   timid, fearful
validus, valida   strong

VERBS

auscultat   (he, she, it) listens (to)
habitat   (he, she, it) lives
narrat   (he, she, it) relates, tells

pugnat   (he, she, it) fights
sunt   they are
terminat   (he, she, it) finishes, ends

OTHER

aut   or
numquam   never
saepe   mostly, generally

semper   always
tempus fugit   time flies

_____ I. QUAESTIŌNĒS _____

A) Did you understand the story? Answer the following questions in English to show that you did.

1. Who is Marcella?

   _____

2. Where does she live?

   _____

3. Who is Lavinia?

   _____

4. Describe Lavinia.

   _____

5. Where are Lavinia and Marcella today?

   _____

6. Who is Trebius?

   _____

7. Who is Vergilius?

   _____

8. Why does Marcella especially like Trebius?

   _____

9. Who is Atticus?

   _____

10. Why doesn't Atticus stay for dinner with Trebius, Marcella, and Lavinia?

    _____

B) There are six Latin sentences below based on the story about Marcella and her mother. To practice using the new vocabulary introduced in this chapter, write two questions for each sentence given:

    a) one question that begins with an interrogative word (*Quis? Quid? Ubi?*) according to the cues given.

    b) one question that requires a yes/no answer.

            EXAMPLE: Marcella est discipula clāra et studiōsa.

                          Quis est discipula?

                          Estne Marcella studiōsa?

1. Marcella in vīllā magnā prope ōceanum habitat.

_____

_____

2. Lāvīnia est māterfamiliās.

_____

_____

3. Lāvīnia vīllam magnam et familiam contentam habet.

_____

_____

4. Marcella in hortō hodiē est.

_____

_____

5. Lāvīnia virum videt prope villam.

_____

_____

6. Trebius fābulam bonam semper narrat.

_____

_____

C) Now translate the 12 questions you just wrote in Exercise B into GOOD English.

1. _____

   _____

2. _____

   _____

3. _____

   _____

4. _____

   _____

5. _____

   _____

6. _____

   _____

CUPID, THE GOD OF LOVE

In Roman mythology, Cupido, the son of Venus and the god of love, used his bow and arrow to shoot love and desire into the hearts of his "victims." Even today, more than 2,000 years later, 20th-century Americans send greetings to loved ones on February 14th that often bear the same, familiar winged child figure still shooting his arrows of love. Cupid has come to represent love, but we can see the root of his name in the Latin adjective *cupidus, cupida* which means "desirous," "eager," "keen."

_____ II. DERIVATIVES _____

A) In Chapter VIII we found that more than 65 percent of all English words come to us from Latin root words. In this chapter, we have learned a number of new vocabulary words. Using your knowledge of Latin vocabulary as well as a little common sense, how many English words can you list that are related to the following Latin words? This is an exercise where the use of a dictionary will probably prove helpful.

1. Latin word: _____ FĒMINA _____

    English meaning: _____ WOMAN _____

    Related English words: _____

    _____

    _____

    _____

    _____

2. Latin word: _____ VIR _____

    English meaning: _____ MAN _____

    Related English words: _____

    _____

    _____

    _____

    _____

3. Latin word: _____ HABITAT _____

    English meaning: _____ (HE, SHE, IT) LIVES _____

    Related English words: _____

    _____

    _____

    _____

    _____

4. Latin word: _____ TERMINAT _____

English meaning: _____ (HE, SHE, IT) ENDS _____

Related English words: _____

_____

_____

_____

_____

_____

B) Here is a list of English words. In the blanks write the Latin word that is from the same family. Choose your answers from the *Index Verbōrum* on page CXLIII or consult a dictionary.

1. _____ occupancy

2. _____ paternity

3. _____ matron

4. _____ affiliation

5. _____ pugnacious

6. _____ captivate

7. _____ filial

8. _____ matrimony

9. _____ valor

10. _____ repugnant

11. _____ valiant

12. _____ patronage

LATIN EXPRESSIONS STILL USED IN MODERN ENGLISH

In addition to the many words that English has borrowed from Latin there are also many Latin expressions that have come down to us intact and unchanged. They are used today in their original forms in everyday English and usually in exactly the same way the Romans used them. A good example is the Latin expression *tempus fugit* from the story about Marcella at the beginning of this chapter.

Here is a list of a few other such Latin expressions. Watch for them in your local newspaper. Now that you're aware of them, you'll be surprised at how often they pop up! See if you can add others to the list!

Expression	Meaning
ad nauseam	to the point of disgust or boredom
in absēntiā	in one's absence
per capita	apiece, for each individual
per sē	by itself
status quō	the existing state of affairs
terra fīrma	solid ground
via	by way of
vice versā	the other way around

For each sentence below, substitute the appropriate Latin expression from the list.

1. The new governor of our state is not interested in making a lot of changes. He favors the _____.
   (SYSTEM AS IT EXISTS)

2. The workers in that country have a _____ income of only $250 per year.
   (INDIVIDUAL)

3. He continued to repeat all the gory details of the accident

   _____.
   (TO THE POINT OF DISGUST)

4. It isn't the contract _____ that is causing the problem, but rather
   (BY ITSELF)
   the way it is being interpreted.

5. Since they had escaped and could not be found, the court tried the couple

   _____ and found them guilty.
   (IN THEIR ABSENCE)

6. After two months in the space station, the astronauts were delighted to set foot once again on _____ .
   (SOLID GROUND)

7. We returned to San Francisco _____ Chicago.
   (BY WAY OF)

8. You can do your homework tonight and go to the movies tomorrow or

   _____ , but you can't go to the movies two nights in a row!
   (THE OTHER WAY AROUND)

LECTIO XI

Verbs Ending in ‑ĀRE: The First Conjugation

STEM   ENDING

I. ANALYSIS EXERCISE

ANALYSIS QUESTION

What is an *infinitive* and what is the meaning of the endings on verbs?

> ### The Verbs
>
> | English | Latin |
> |---|---|
> | to love | amāre |
> | to place/to put | locāre |
> | to carry | portāre |
> | to hit | pulsāre |

A) Look at the four Latin verbs above. What are the last two letters of each verb?

_____

A Latin verb that has this ending is called an **infinitive.**

Amāre, locāre, portāre, and *pulsāre* are **infinitives.**

Latin **infinitives** are made up of a *stem* and an *ending*:

The *stem* portion carries the basic meaning of the word:

amā	=	love
locā	=	place/put
portā	=	carry
pulsā	=	hit

By adding the -re ending to the stem, we create the *infinitive*:

amāre	=	to love
locāre	=	to place, to put
portāre	=	to carry
pulsāre	=	to hit

B) Look at the four English verbs you just read. What two-letter word precedes each verb?

_____

> ## NOTĀ BENE
>
> In English the **infinitive** form of the verb is composed of the word **to** plus the verb.
>
> **To** love, **to** place, **to** put, **to** carry, **to** hit are **infinitives.**
>
> The Latin verb **portāre** means *to carry* and not just *carry* alone. **Pulsāre** means *to hit*, not just *hit*, etc.

C) We've mixed some English and Latin verbs in the following list. Circle each verb that is in the "infinitive form" (both Latin and English infinitives, please). All the *Latin* verbs are in italics to help you spot them.

to eat	to write	*locāre*	to go
run	*laborāre*	are	goes
amāre	*sunt*	holds	*lavat*
portāre	cry	*loco*	*teneo*
portat	*habēre*	*amat*	share
est	to hold		

D) Of course, we have already been using some verbs in Latin. Remember these sentences from Quintus Caecilius's mischievous caper with the frog?

Clēmens urnam portat.
Prope mūrum Clēmens urnam locat.

Let's take a closer look at these verbs now and do a little analyzing.

Portat and *locat* are NOT infinitives since they do NOT end in

_____ .

CONCLUSION

Portat does NOT mean *to carry* and **locat** does NOT mean *to put*.

The stem of *portāre* is _____ .

The stem of *locāre* is _____ .

Did you remember to include the *macron* to signal a long ā?

CONCLUSION

Portat and *locat* seem to be composed of a verb stem plus the letter

_____ .

What happened to the long ā in *portat* and *locat*?

_____

Look up the meaning of the two verbs (*portat* and *locat*) in the *Index Verbōrum* at the end of the book and copy the English meaning in the spaces below.

portat: _____

locat: _____

CONCLUSION

The letter *t* on the end of a Latin verb seems to have three meanings in English:

_____ , _____ , or _____

E) Using what you just learned in parts *A*, *B*, and *C* of Part D, can you translate these verbs if you are given the meaning of the following Latin infinitives?

Here are the verbs and their English meanings:

pugnāre	= to fight	**auscultāre**	= to listen (to)
cōgitāre	= to think	**narrāre**	= to relate, to tell
labōrāre	= to work, toil	**vocāre**	= to call, to invite
habitāre	= to live	**spectāre**	= to watch, to look at
vīsitāre	= to visit	**termināre**	= to finish, to end
vulnerāre	= to wound	**parāre**	= to prepare

Try these, from Latin to English:

1. spectat: _____

2. labōrat: _____

3. vocat: _____

4. auscultat: _____

5. narrat: _____

How about the other way around, from English to Latin?

6. he visits: _____

7. she finishes: _____

8. he lives: _____

9. she thinks: _____

10. it wounds: _____

What if we add a proper name before the verb?

11. Quintus vocat: _____

12. Trebius terminat: _____

13. Atticus pugnat: _____

14. Publius vulnerat: _____

15. Marcus parat: _____

And finally, what happens when we put a girl's name in front of the verb?

16. Marcia vīsitat: _____

17. Marcella auscultat: _____

18. Virginia cōgitat: _____

19. Lāvīnia habitat: _____

Taking into account all of what we learned in the exercise we just finished, what can we conclude? Write *true* or *false* in the blanks.

CONCLUSION

1. The letter *t* on the end of a Latin verb should be translated as *he, she,* or *it* depending on whether the subject of the sentence is a man (masculine), a woman (feminine), or a thing (neuter).

   _____

2. Where there is a noun in the nominative case in the sentence, that **noun** should be translated as the subject instead of *he, she,* or *it.*

Puella cōgitat.	The girl thinks.
Puer labōrat.	The boy works.
Asinus auscultat.	The donkey listens.
Marcella terminat.	Marcella finishes.

   _____

Will the real "I" please stand up?

THE CONCEPT OF "PERSON" WHEN TALKING ABOUT VERBS

So far, so good. But before we continue, we've got to come to some agreement about the meaning of a few terms.

Suppose that we were having a conversation, just the two of us, you and I. When *I* am doing the talking, I refer to myself as "I," and at that moment, I hold the position of importance in our conversation because I am the communicator. *You* (the listener), then, hold the position of second importance in our conversation. If we talked about anybody or anything else (*he, she,* or *it*), they would be third in importance.

On the other hand, when *you* are doing the talking, you also refer to yourself as "I" and *you* hold the position of importance in the conversation during the time that you are talking.

Therefore, when *I* say "I," I mean *me* (the teacher). When *you* say "I," you mean *you* (the student). It is quite clear that unless we agree on some basic terminology, we can get pretty confused as to who "I" is.

NOTĀ BENE

I is the **first person** (that is, whoever is doing the talking).

You is the **second person** (whoever is doing the listening).

He, she, it is the **third person** (the person or object about whom we are talking).

singular   Plural

The Concept of "Number" When Talking about Verbs

1. In addition, the first, second, and third persons also have plural counterparts. When I talk about *myself* ("I") plus anybody else, I refer to the group as "we." Therefore, "I" is the *first person singular* and "we" is the *first person plural*.

    > *My brothers and I get along well.*
    > *We* went to the movies last night.

2. Second person singular *you* does not change its form in the plural. It remains *you*. In the sentence below, the first *you* is singular, but the second *you* is plural.

    > I want to talk to *you* (John) while *you* (the rest of the class) study quietly at your desks.

3. The plural form of *he, she,* or *it* is *they*.

Conclusion

It is convenient, when talking about verbs, to refer to the **person** and the **number** of a verb.

Person refers to *first, second,* or *third* persons (i.e., who is performing the action of the verb from the point of view of the speaker).

Number refers to *singular* or *plural* (i.e., the number of persons performing the action of the verb).

II. ANALYSIS EXERCISE

THE CONCEPT OF "CONJUGATION"

ANALYSIS QUESTION

What does *conjugation* mean and what are *personal endings*?

When we list all of the forms of a verb (all of the possible persons who can perform the action described by the verb) we say that we are *conjugating* that verb. Here is the full *conjugation* of the verb *to carry* in English and in Latin. *To carry* is a verb of the *first conjugation* in Latin.

MODEL OF A FIRST CONJUGATION VERB

portō, portāre (to carry)

	SINGULAR			PLURAL	
First person:	portō	= I carry	portāmus	= we carry
Second person:	portās	= you (singular) carry	portātis	= you (plural) carry
Third person:	portat	= he, she, it carries	portant	= they carry

---

NOTĀ BENE

In a Latin dictionary, a verb is always listed by its first person singular form followed by the infinitive form (portō, portāre). Two other forms are also usually given. In a Latin dictionary, the verb *to carry* would be listed like this:

portō, portāre, portāvī, portātus

These are the **four principal parts** of the verb *to carry*. For the time being you will be expected to know only the first two principal parts of each of the verbs we study. We will see later how the others help us to identify more Latin derivatives.

A) Referring to the conjugation of *portō*, *portāre*, answer these questions. Write your answer in the blank on the left.

1. _____ Counting the infinitive form, how many times does the word *carry* appear in the English conjugation?

2. _____ How many times does the word *carries* appear in the English conjugation?

3. _____ If we took away the personal pronouns (*I*, *you*, *we*, *they*) and left only the verb form (*carry*), would you be able to tell WHO was *carrying*?

CONCLUSION

In English, the personal pronoun that precedes the verb is an important element of the sentence and cannot be omitted (except, of course, when it is replaced by the *noun* it represents: John, Jane, the children, for example). (Write *true* or *false* in the blank below.)

_____

B) Referring again to the conjugation of *portō*, *portāre*, answer these questions. Write your answer in the blank on the left.

1. _____ Including the infinitive form, are there any two words that are exactly alike in the Latin conjugation?

2. _____ If I said the word *portāmus*, would you be able to determine WHO was *carrying*?

CHARIOTS—A DAY AT THE RACES

Chariot racing was one of the Romans' favorite spectator sports. In fact, they loved it so much that it was not uncommon for spectators to witness anywhere from 12 to 24 races in a single day! The races took place in special stadiums called *circuses* that were built especially for this purpose. The *Circus Maximus* was the most famous and the largest of the Roman circuses. It was so big that it could seat more than 250,000 spectators at one time.

A race in the circus consisted of seven laps around the track. Each chariot was drawn by a team of horses—two to six horses per team. Sometimes dog, camel, or even teams of ostriches were used to pull the chariots. Charioteers who repeatedly won the races against their fellow drivers became famous and amassed huge fortunes as well as the adoration of their fans.

Today, huge crowds still thrill at the competition of motorized "chariots" that race in the Indianapolis 500 and the French *Grand Prix.* Perhaps a more direct descendant of chariot racing, however, is harness racing.

C) Look again at the Latin conjugation of *to carry*. The underlined letters are the *personal endings*. Each personal ending represents a different person. (Therefore, a separate pronoun is not needed.)

You have already met up with the **-t** of *portat*, which means *he*, *she*, or *it*. Checking with the Latin conjugation of *portō*, *portāre*, and the English translation given, fill in the English meanings of each of the *personal endings* listed below.

PERSONAL ENDING	ENGLISH MEANING
-ō	_____
-s	_____
-t	he, she, it (Jack, Jill, the pail)
-mus	_____
-tis	_____
-nt	they (Jack and Jill)

D) Taking another look at the Latin conjugation of *to carry*, answer these questions.

1. Write the infinitive form of the verb here:

_____

2. Write the stem of the verb here:

_____

3. Notice that the stem of *portāre* ends in the letter

_____

This is characteristic of all verbs of the first conjugation.

4. Write the first person singular form of the verb here:

_____

5. What happens to the ā from the stem of *portāre*?

_____

6. Does the *a* appear in the rest of the conjugation of *portāre*?

_____

7. Is the *a* a long *ā* in all of the forms of the conjugation?

_____

8. Write the two forms of the verb where the long *ā* becomes a short *a*.

_____

E) Write the Analysis Question in the space below, then fill in the blanks to complete the conclusion and to summarize what you have learned about the first conjugation.

_____

CONCLUSION

1. When we list all the forms of a verb (all the possible persons) we say that

we are _____ that verb.

2. Latin verbs of the first conjugation are characterized by the

letter _____ (long or short) which appears in all of its

forms except the _____ person singular (*portō*).

3. The *personal endings* on the verbs represent different persons. Therefore,

separate pronouns _____ needed.
      (ARE/ARE NOT)

4. When the personal ending -*ō* is used, it means that *I* is the subject of the
verb. If the personal ending -*s* is added to the stem, it means that *you*
(singular) is the subject of the verb, etc.

portō	means	*I carry*
portant	means	*they carry*
vocat	means	*he (or she or it) calls*
Marcus vocat	means	*Mark calls*
labōrō	means	*I work*
labōrāmus	means	*we work*

F) Now go back to the conjugation of *portō, portāre* on page CLVIII and draw a box around the ending (and only the ending, please) of each form of the verb.

G) There are 12 verbs listed below. You probably recognize some of them because you have been using them in their third person singular form in the exercises throughout this book. All of them are *first conjugation verbs*.

Now that you have learned how to conjugate them, you can use them in many more ways than before. Make sure you know the meaning of each verb, then go on to do the exercises that follow.

INDEX VERBŌRUM

FIRST CONJUGATION VERBS

(ambulat)	**ambulō, ambulāre**	=	to walk
(amat)	**amō, amāre**	=	to love
(auscultat)	**auscultō, auscultāre**	=	to listen (to)
(clāmat)	**clāmō, clāmāre**	=	to call, to shout
(habitat)	**habitō, habitāre**	=	to live
(lacrimat)	**lacrimō, lacrimāre**	=	to cry, to weep
(locat)	**locō, locāre**	=	to place, to put
(narrat)	**narrō, narrāre**	=	to relate, to tell
(portat)	**portō, portāre**	=	to carry
(pugnat)	**pugnō, pugnāre**	=	to fight
(pulsat)	**pulsō, pulsāre**	=	to hit, to strike
(terminat)	**terminō, termināre**	=	to finish, to end

_____ III. EXERCITĀTIŌNĒS _____

A) Each of the following sentences needs a verb to complete its meaning. Add the proper form of the verb as indicated, then translate the whole sentence into GOOD English.

1. Quintum et Titum _____ . (she loves)

    _____

2. Prope librum chartam _____ _____ . (you, *singular*, put)

    _____

3. Aquam prope lacum _____ . (I listen to)

    _____

4. Agricolam _____ . (you, *plural*, hit)

    _____

5. Taurum magnum in harēnā _____ . (we fight)

    _____

6. In hortō _____ . (they walk)

    _____

7. Terram bonam _____ . (we love)

    _____

8. Discipulum clārum _____ . (you, *singular*, call)

    _____

9. Puer et puella urnam magnam _____ . (they carry)

    _____

10. Puer et puella _____ . (they cry)

    _____

B) In the exercise below, each verb has been reduced to its stem minus the *a*. (See the verb list on page CLXIII.) For each sentence, decide if the *a* is needed or not. If it is, add the *a* (a long *ā* or a short *a*) as well as the proper personal ending in order to complete the sentence as indicated. If the *a* is not needed, then just add the proper personal ending to complete the sentence correctly.

In the blanks on the left, write the *person* (1, 2, or 3) and *number* (S or P) of each verb.

Don't forget, the personal ending is always added to the full *stem* of the verb except in the *first person singular*, where the *a* of the stem is dropped.

Leave the line under each Latin sentence blank for the moment.

PERSON NUMBER

_____ _____   **1.** Librum am _____ (we)

_____

_____ _____   **2.** Discipulum clām _____ (you, *plural*)

_____

_____ _____   **3.** Papȳrum semper port _____ (I)

_____

_____ _____   **4.** Equum puls _____ (you, *singular*)

_____

_____ _____   **5.** Quaestiōnem termin _____ (they)

_____

_____ _____   **6.** Fābulam longam narr _____ (Iūlia)

_____

_____ _____   **7.** Rānam prope lectum loc _____ (she)

_____

_____ _____   **8.** Lacrim _____ (you, *plural*)

_____

_____ _____   **9.** Cibum par _____ (Marcus et Gāius)

_____

_____ _____ **10.** Magistrum auscult _____ (servus)

_____

_____ _____ **11.** Crētam prope urbam loc _____ (they)

_____

_____ _____ **12.** Magistrum am _____ (I)

_____

C) Study the 12 sentences in Part B, which you just finished, then complete the statements below.

1. In each of the 12 sentences (except for the eighth), the first word of the sentence is in the same case. Which one?

    _____

    This indicates that these words are the _____ of the sentences.

2. What is the subject of the first sentence? (give in English)

    _____

3. What is the subject of the second sentence? (give in English)

    _____

4. How are the subjects of the first and second sentences represented in the Latin sentences?

    _____

5. What is the infinitive form of the verb in the first sentence? (In Latin, please.)

    _____

6. What is the infinitive form of the verb in the second sentence? (In Latin, also.)

    _____

D) Now go back to Part B and translate each sentence into GOOD English on the line provided.

Index Verbōrum

Here is a list of useful *first conjugation* verbs. The conjugation of each of these verbs is exactly like the conjugation of *portō, portāre*. First, you find the stem of the verb by cutting off the **-re** ending from the infinitive, and then you add the same personal endings to change the person. Be careful of the irregularity in the first person singular form, though.

ambulō, ambulāre   to walk
amō, amāre   to love
auscultō, auscultāre   to listen (to)
cēnō, cēnāre   to dine, to have dinner
clāmō, clāmāre   to call, to shout
cōgitō, cōgitāre   to think
gustō, gustāre   to taste
habitō, habitāre   to live
intrō, intrāre (followed by *in + accusative*) to enter, to walk into
labōrō, labōrāre   to work, to toil
lacrimō, lacrimāre   to cry, to weep
laudō, laudāre   to praise

narrō, narrāre   to relate, to tell
parō, parāre   to prepare
portō, portāre   to carry
pugnō, pugnāre   to fight
pulsō, pulsāre   to strike, to hit
salutō, salutāre   to greet
spectō, spectāre   to look at, to watch
terminō, termināre   to finish, to end
vīsitō, vīsitāre   to visit
vocō, vocāre   to call, to invite
vulnerō, vulnerāre   to wound, to injure

E)   Supply the missing forms of the verbs given below to complete the conjugation. Make sure that the ORDER is correct. Study the example carefully before you begin.

EXAMPLE: ____PULSŌ____, ____PULSĀRE____ (____TO HIT____)

PULSŌ	PULSĀMUS
PULSĀS	PULSĀTIS
PULSAT	PULSANT

1. ____SALUTŌ____, _____ (_____)

_____ _____

_____ _____

_____ _____

NŌMEN_____

DIĒS_____

2. _____, _____ (_____)

_____ _____

_____ _____ LABŌRĀTIS _____

_____ _____

3. _____, _____ (_____)

_____ _____

_____ _____

_____ CŌGITAT _____ _____

4. _____ _____ _____ TO WALK INTO _____

_____ _____

_____ _____

_____ _____

F) Indicate in the blanks on the left the *person* (1, 2, or 3) and *number* (S or P) of each expression given, then translate each of them into Latin.

PERSON NUMBER   ENGLISH   LATIN TRANSLATION

____ ____ **1.** they think   _____

____ ____ **2.** we taste   _____

____ ____ **3.** you (*plural*) enter   _____

____ ____ **4.** I listen   _____

____ ____ **5.** we watch   _____

____ ____ **6.** she tells   _____

____ ____ **7.** I look at   _____

____ ____ **8.** you (*singular*) greet _____

NŌMEN _____

DIĒS _____

_____ _____ **9.** Trebius eats dinner _____

_____ _____ **10.** we walk _____

_____ _____ **11.** they live _____

_____ _____ **12.** he injures _____

_____ _____ **13.** we cry _____

_____ _____ **14.** Melissa and Anna praise _____

G) In each of the sentences below, circle the verb, underline its personal ending, then translate the sentence into GOOD English. In the blank at the left, indicate the *person*. Be sure to check the *Index Verbōrum* at the back of the book for any vocabulary you may not know.

_____ **1.** Prope aquam Quintus et Cornēlia cenant.

_____

_____ **2.** Cibum gustātis.

_____

_____ **3.** Puella clāra cōgitat.

_____

_____ **4.** Tiberius in Graeciā habitat.

_____

_____ **5.** Claudiam et fēminam Hispānam salutāmus.

_____

_____ **6.** Aemilia fēminam nōn vocat.

_____

_____ **7.** Intrantne in hortum ūmidum?

_____

_____ **8.** Cornēliam captīvus inimīcus vulnerat.

_____

_____ **9.** Cōgitās.

_____

_____ **10.** Servum et servam auscultātis.

_____

H) Try your hand at translating these sentences from English to Latin. Use the *Index Verbōrum* at the end of the book for words you may not know. Be especially careful of the verbs and their endings, and don't forget the difference between *nominative* and *accusative!* Make sure to place your verb last.

1. The man greets the woman.

_____

2. Lavinia loves the house near the ocean.

_____

3. Mark or Paul always visit the family.

_____

4. I watch the pleasant servant girl. She works in the kitchen.

_____

5. The gladiator fights the bull in the arena.

_____

6. They greet Valeria. She visits a very good friend today.

_____

LECTIO XII

Verbs Ending in ‑ĒRE:
The Second Conjugation

RĪDĒRE

I. ANALYSIS EXERCISE

ANALYSIS QUESTION

How do we conjugate a second conjugation verb?

MODEL OF A SECOND CONJUGATION VERB

habeō, habēre (to have)

	SINGULAR		PLURAL
1st person:	habeō = I have	habēmus	= we have
2nd person:	habēs = you (singular) have	habētis	= you (plural) have
3rd person:	habet = he, she, it has	habent	= they have

REVIEW AND COMPARISON

Compare the forms of this verb with the verb conjugated on page CLVIII, then answer the questions.

1. Write the infinitive form of both verbs in the blanks below.

    _____   _____

2. Write the stem of both verbs.

    _____   _____

3. The stem of *portāre* ends in the letter _____.

    We already know that this letter is characteristic of the _____
    conjugation.   (FIRST/SECOND/THIRD)

4. The stem of *habēre* ends in the letter _____.
    This letter is characteristic of the second conjugation.

5. Write the *first person singular* form of both verbs here:

    _____   _____

    a) What happens to the ā from the stem of portāre?

        _____

    b) What about the ē from the stem of *habēre*?

        _____

    c) Does the *a* (long and short) appear in the rest of the conjugation of *portāre*?

        _____

    d) How about the *e* (long and short) in *habēre*?

        _____

    e) Are the personal endings the *same* or *different* for these two verbs? (Check the whole conjugation of each to make sure.)

        _____

    f) Draw a box around the ending (the ending only) of each form of the verb *habeō*, *habēre* in the box at the beginning of this chapter.

LET'S SUMMARIZE WHAT WE HAVE LEARNED

The First Conjugation

Latin verbs of the first conjugation are characterized by a long *a* in their infinitive forms and either a long or short *a* in all their other forms. There is one exception: the first person singular (portō, for example).

The Second Conjugation

Latin verbs of the second conjugation are characterized by a long *e* in their infinitive forms and either a long or short *e* in all their other forms.

The Other Conjugations

Latin verbs are grouped into *four* conjugations. We will concentrate on the *first* and *second* conjugations in this course.

Chariot racing was a favorite spectator sport of the Romans.

_____ II. EXERCITĀTIŌNĒS _____

INDEX VERBŌRUM

Here is a list of useful *second conjugation* verbs. Each verb on this list conjugates like the model verb in the Analysis Exercise on page CLXXI (that is, by adding the same personal endings to the stem). Study this list before you begin the exercises on the following pages.

habeō, habēre	to have	**rīdeō, rīdēre**	to laugh, to smile
moneō, monēre	to warn, to advise	**sedeō, sedēre**	to sit
moveō, movēre	to move	**teneō, tenēre**	to hold
prōvideō, prōvidēre	to provide, to foresee	**terreō, terrēre**	to frighten
respondeō, respondēre	to reply, to answer	**videō, vidēre**	to see

A) Each of the following sentences needs a verb to complete its meaning. Add the proper form of the verb as indicated, then translate the whole sentence into GOOD English.

1. Librum optimum _____.
   (SHE HAS)

   _____

2. Minimē, tunicam albam prope sellam nōn _____.
   (YOU, *SINGULAR*, SEE)

   _____

3. Quintus et Marius fēminam Hispānam _____.
   (THEY WARN)

   _____

4. Stilum et tabellam _____.
   (I PROVIDE)

   _____

5. Gladium magnum et fāmōsum _____.
   (YOU, *PLURAL*, HOLD)

   _____

6. Captīvum barbarum _____.
   (WE DO NOT FRIGHTEN)

   _____

NŌMEN _____

DIĒS _____

7. Prope fenestram cathēdram _____.
    (I MOVE)

8. Proserpina et Cornēlia numquam _____.
    (THEY ANSWER)

9. Ubi _____?
    (WE SIT)

10. Ita, semper _____.
    (YOU, *SINGULAR*, LAUGH)

B) In this list, we've mixed first and second conjugation verbs together. Can you sort them out? Indicate in the blanks on the left the *conjugation* of the verb (first or second), then tell what *person* and what *number* each verb is. Finally, translate the expression given into Latin.

CONJUGATION	PERSON	NUMBER	ENGLISH	LATIN TRANSLATION
____	____	____	1. I sit	_____
____	____	____	2. Aemilia praises	_____
____	____	____	3. Anna and Marcia have	_____
____	____	____	4. We watch	_____
____	____	____	5. You, *singular*, enter	_____
____	____	____	6. I listen	_____
____	____	____	7. you, *plural*, see	_____
____	____	____	8. the boy lives	_____
____	____	____	9. he replies	_____
____	____	____	10. we provide	_____
____	____	____	11. we hold	_____
████	____	____	12. he is	_____

C) In each of the sentences below, circle the verb(s) and then determine to which conjugation it belongs. Write *1* or *2* in the space on the left, then translate each sentence into GOOD English.

_____ 1. Rīdēmus et cenam bonam parāmus.

_____ _____

_____ 2. Claudia in Italiā cum familiā habitat.

_____

_____ 3. Quintus et Marcus puellam parvam numquam terrent.

_____

_____ 4. Virginia harēnam in aquā nōn videt.

_____

_____ 5. Claudius chartam et tabellam portat sed stilum nōn habēmus.

_____ _____

_____

_____ 6. Taurus et asinus rānam parvam spectant.

_____

_____ 7. Gallum saepe tenēs.

_____

_____ 8. Drūsīlla et Matella virum prōcērum salutant.

_____

_____ 9. Cenāmus sed cibum nōn amāmus.

_____ _____

_____

_____ 10. Caesar in vīllam intrat et populum salutat.

_____ _____

_____

_____ 11. Populus Rōmānus cibum bonum amat.

_____

_____ **12.** Decimus tabulam Lātinam in scholā tenet sed in vīllā tabulam Lātinam numquam habet.

_____   _____

            _____

D) Read the *instruction maze* below and do what it says.

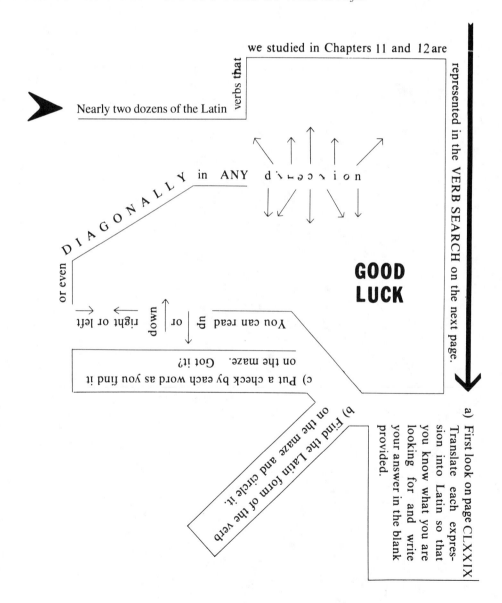

Nearly two dozens of the Latin verbs **that** we studied in Chapters 11 and 12 are represented in the VERB SEARCH on the next page.

a) First look on page CLXXIX. Translate each expression into Latin so that you know what you are looking for and write your answer in the blank provided.

b) Find the Latin form of the verb on the maze and circle it.

c) Put a check by each word as you find it on the maze. Got it?

You can read up or down or right or left DIAGONALLY or even in ANY direction

GOOD LUCK

VERB SEARCH

```
V  I  S  I  T  A  R  E  A  L  O  M  T  A  C
E  L  V  I  T  A  M  M  R  N  P  O  R  T  O
T  A  L  H  A  B  E  O  E  A  L  V  L  I  G
S  B  R  A  L  C  S  N  M  O  R  E  M  R  I
I  O  R  B  T  A  S  E  S  V  U  T  U  A  T
T  R  E  E  T  R  U  M  O  V  E  C  N  R  O
E  A  R  C  R  O  M  U  R  A  T  I  O  I  S
D  T  E  O  A  T  E  S  A  L  U  T  A  T  I
E  P  I  G  S  R  T  G  F  R  O  T  O  R  T
S  S  I  T  E  D  I  V  U  E  S  A  H  I  E
H  A  B  N  T  R  U  L  V  S  A  E  R  D  D
A  R  E  S  L  A  U  D  O  P  T  R  A  E  I
B  T  S  U  M  A  N  E  C  E  R  A  S  R  V
I  M  A  R  O  C  R  G  O  T  A  N  N  E  O
T  U  M  A  R  E  S  P  O  N  D  E  O  T  R
O  V  A  T  N  E  R  R  E  T  E  C  E  L  P
```

_____ **1.** I have   _____

_____ **2.** we warn   _____

_____ **3.** to hold   _____

_____ **4.** you, *plural*, see   _____

_____ **5.** he greets   _____

_____ **6.** to enter   _____

_____ **7.** you, *singular*, watch   _____

_____ **8.** they taste   _____

_____ **9.** I praise   _____

_____ **10.** she moves   _____

_____ **11.** you, *plural*, sit   _____

_____ **12.** to laugh   _____

_____ **13.** I call   _____

_____ **14.** to visit   _____

_____ **15.** we dine   _____

_____ **16.** I live   _____

_____ **17.** he works   _____

_____ **18.** I carry   _____

_____ **19.** you, *singular*, love   _____

_____ **20.** I think   _____

_____ **21.** to dine   _____

_____ **22.** I answer   _____

_____ **23.** you, *plural*, provide   _____

_____ **24.** they frighten   _____

INDEX VERBŌRUM

Use the new vocabulary below to help you do the exercises that follow.

NOUNS

arbor (*accusative* = arborem)   **populus**   people
  f. tree   **pūpa**   doll
fluvius   stream, river   **sciūrus**   squirrel
Graecia   Greece

ADJECTIVES

antīquus, antīqua   old, ancient   **splendidus, splendida**
  (applied to *things* but not to   splendid, magnificent
  people)   **timidus, timida**   timid, fearful
fuscus, fusca   dark, black   **tranquillus, tranquilla**   calm,
                                            quiet

OTHER

Ecce!   Here is! There is!   **semper**   always
  Behold!

E) Translate the following sentences into GOOD English.

1. Pūpam antīquam tenet Claudius. Laetus est.

    _____

    _____

2. Decimus aut Aemilius sciūrum parvum fuscum habet. Sciūrus est timidus.

    _____

    _____

3. In culīnā semper cēnāmus sed cibus bonus numquam est.

    _____

    _____

4. Cicero populum Rōmānum salutat. Caesar in Graeciā est.

    _____

    _____

5. Arbor prope fluvium tranquillum est. Magna et splendida est.

_____

_____

6. Ecce, vīlla magna! Vīllam splendidam vidēmus.

_____

_____

7. Mandūcus arborem antiquam spectat. Splendida est!

_____

_____

A SPECIAL CATEGORY OF ADJECTIVES: POSSESSIVE ADJECTIVES

"Possessive" adjectives are, naturally enough, adjectives that indicate "possession." In English, words like *my, our, your, his,* and *her* are possessive adjectives.

We've already learned that in Latin, adjectives agree with the nouns they modify in gender and case. Well, possessive adjectives, like other adjectives, also agree with

the nouns they modify in _____ and _____. Here is a list of Latin possessive adjectives.

POSSESSIVE ADJECTIVES

NOMINATIVE		ACCUSATIVE		
Masculine	Feminine	Masculine	Feminine	
meus	**mea**	**meum**	**meam**	= my
noster	**nostra**	**nostrum**	**nostram**	= our
tuus	**tua**	**tuum**	**tuam**	= your (*singular*)
vester	**vestra**	**vestrum**	**vestram**	= your (*plural*)
suus	**sua**	**suum**	**suam**	= his or her (*own*)

DON'T LET A POSSESSIVE ADJECTIVE TRIP YOU UP: A WORD OF CAUTION

Actually, using possessive adjectives is no different from using a regular adjective in Latin. However, there is one little problem that pops up for English speakers and the problem exists because of the way we use the possessive adjectives *his* and *her* in English. Look at the following examples.

How It Works in English

In English, we choose a masculine or feminine possessive adjective based on the gender of the *possessor*. The question we must ask ourself is: Is the gender of the *person who does the possessing* masculine or feminine?

> Atticus is a gladiator.
> > *His* sword is big.
> > *His* tunic is white.

We choose the possessive adjective *his* when talking about Atticus's sword and tunic because *Atticus* (the *possessor* of those items) is masculine. It doesn't matter what the gender of *sword* or *tunic* is.

> Maria is a girl.
> > *Her* doll is pretty.
> > *Her* father is strong.

We choose the possessive adjective *her* when talking about Maria's garden and house because *Maria* (the *possessor* of those things) is feminine. Again, it doesn't matter what the gender of *garden* or *house* is.

How It Works in Latin

In Latin, however, the choice of a masculine or feminine possessive adjective is based on the gender of the *thing possessed* and not the possessor. The question we must ask ourselves in Latin is: Is the *object that is possessed* masculine or feminine? Look at the same examples translated into Latin and watch the gender of the possessive adjective change.

> Atticus est gladiator.
> > Gladius *suus* est magnus.
> > Tunica *sua* est alba.

> Maria est puella.
> > Pūpa *sua* est formōsa.
> > Pater *suus* est validus.

Actually, this is exactly the way all adjectives work in Latin: the adjective agrees with the noun it describes.

> Suus can mean either *his* or *her*.
> Sua can also mean either *his* or *her*.

REMEMBER

In Latin, your choice of which form to use (*suus* or *sua*) depends on the gender of the word the adjective describes (or, put another way, it depends on the gender of the *thing possessed*).

In English, your choice of translation (*his* or *her*) depends on the gender of the *possessor*.

III. EXERCITĀTIŌNĒS

A) Fill in the blank with the correct form of the appropriate possessive adjective, then translate your sentence into GOOD English. Use the *Index Verbōrum* at the back of the book to find the meaning of any words you may not know.

1. Claudia amīca _____ bona est. Familia _____ in
   (MY) (HER)
   casā prope fluvium habitat.

   _____

   _____

2. Ecce Pugnax! Agricola est. Fīlius _____ semper occupātus
   (HIS)

   est et fīlia _____ studiōsa et clāra est.
   (HIS)

   _____

   _____

3. Vocāmus sed magister _____ nōn respondet. Respondetne
   (OUR)

   grammaticum _____?
   (YOUR, PLURAL)

   _____

   _____

4. Servus _____ et serva _____ in culīnā cibum parant.
   (OUR)   (OUR)

   _____

   _____

5. Amīcus _____, Rufus, patrem _____ in Galliā vīsitat.
   (MY)   (HIS)

   Pater _____ fābulam splendidam narrat.
   (HIS)

   _____

   _____

6. Captīvus validus hodiē tranquillus est sed cibum _____ et
   (HIS)

   aquam _____ nōn gustat.
   (HIS)

   _____

   _____

7. Iūlius est vir honestus. Cibum _____ prōvidet.
   (OUR)

   _____

   _____

8. Theodorus magister Graecus est sed in Graeciā nōn habitat. Fīlia _____
   (HIS)

   nōn est discipula in scholā _____.
   (HIS)

   _____

   _____

B) Circle each possessive adjective and underline all of the other adjectives in the following sentences. Then translate each sentence into Latin. Be careful to use the correct gender and case for all of your adjectives and make sure your word order follows "normal" Latin word order. Use the *Index Verbōrum* at the back of the book to find the translation of any words you may not know.

1. I greet your son. He is a handsome Roman boy.

   _____

   _____

2. Here is your pen but we don't see your book.

   _____

3. Secunda visits our family. We listen to her story and we laugh!

   _____

   _____

4. I call your faithful servant but she doesn't answer. I sit by my window and I watch the road. Now I see her little son. Where is Gaia?

   _____

   _____

   _____

5. A big black squirrel is in my bed!

   _____

6. You answer your mother and you always laugh. Where is your little doll today?

   _____

   _____

LECTIO XIII

Pugnax, Familia, et Cēna Splendida

Fābula

Index Verbōrum

asparagus, asparagōs (accusative plural)   asparagus
coquus   cook, chef
fungus, fungōs (accusative plural)   mushroom
oliva, olivās (accusative plural)   olive
Salvē!   Hello! Greetings!
senātor, senātōrem (accusative)   senator
trīclīnium (neuter), **trīclīnium** (accusative)   dining-room, dining couch

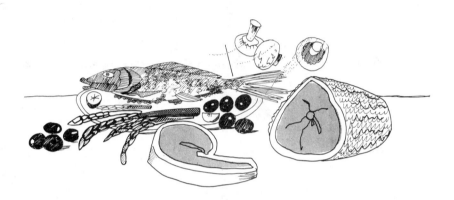

Notā Bene

	2nd Declension *Masculine* noun	2nd Declension *Neuter* noun
Nominative	Amīc**us**	Trīclīni**um**
Accusative	Amīc**um**	Trīclīni**um**
Ablative	Amīc**ō**	Trīclīni**ō**

Look at the declension of the two nouns above. We're already familiar with *amīcus*, a second declension **MASCULINE** noun; but *trīclīnium* is a second declension **NEUTER** noun.

Notice that the nominative case ending of *trīclīnium* is the same as (circle one):

1. the nominative case ending of **AMĪCUS**.
2. the nominative case ending of a feminine noun.
3. the accusative case ending of **TRĪCLĪNIUM**.
4. the accusative case ending of a feminine noun.

It's a good idea to keep this in mind and to remember that **TRĪCLĪNIUM** is a *neuter* noun.

1. Ecce Pugnax! Quis est? Pugnax est servus in vīllā. Servus est contentus. Familia sua bona est.

2. Pugnax in culīnā labōrat. Coquus est. Rōmānus nōn est sed Graecus. Pugnax coquus bonus est et hodiē cēnam magnam parat.

3. Tempus fugit. Cibus parātus nōn est. Porcīnam, asparagōs, fungōs, et olīvās parat Pugnax. Servus labōrat et gustat.

4. Ecce Caecilius, paterfamiliās! In vīllā suā hodiē est.

5. Māterfamiliās est Calpurnia. Calpurnia in vīllā etiaḿ est.

6. Titus Claudius Vērus est amīcus. Caecilium et Calpurniam vīsitat. Prōcērus et formōsus est Claudius. Claudius est senātor Rōmānus. Populus Rōmānus Claudium amat. Claudius in vīllam hodiē intrat.

7. "Salvē!" Claudius Caecilium
salūtat. "Salvē!" respondet
Caecilius.

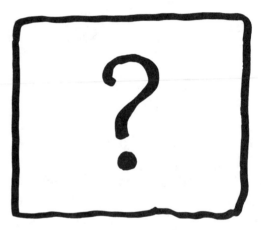

8. "Ubi est Quintus, fīlius tuus?"
Quintus hodiē in vīllā nōn est.

9. Claudius Calpurniam videt.
Calpurniam etiam salūtat.

10. Calpurnia in culīnam intrat.
"Estne cibus parātus?" Pugnax est
fatīgātus. "Ita, est," respondet
Pugnax. Calpurnia contenta est.
Coquus est bonus.

11. Calpurnia in trīclīnium
intrat et Claudium vocat.

12. Caecilius etiam in trīclīnium
intrat. "Estne parāta cēna?"

13. Claudius, Caecilius, et Calpurnia cēnant et rīdent. Cēnam bonam amant. Cēna splendida est. Semper splendida est. Coquum laudant. Coquus nōn est bonus sed optimus!

14. Ubi est Pugnax? In culīnā etiam est. Labōratne coquus bonus? Minimē, nōn labōrat. Sedet. Contentus et tranquillus est sed etiam est fatīgātus.

_____ **I. QUAESTIŌNĒS** _____

A) Answer in English the following questions based on the *fābula*.

1. Translate the title of the story on the line below.

_____

2. Who is Pugnax?

_____

3. Is Pugnax a Roman citizen?

_____

4. What is Pugnax's problem today?

_____

5. What is Pugnax preparing for dinner?

_____

6. Who is Caecilius?

_____

7. Where is Calpurnia today?

_____

8. Who is Claudius?

_____

9. What is Claudius's full name?

_____

10. How does Claudius greet Caecilius when he arrives?

_____

   If *salvē* means *hello*, what do you suppose *valē* means?

_____

11. What does Calpurnia ask Pugnax? (In English, please.)

_____

12. Does Pugnax finish the dinner in time?

_____

13. Where do the diners eat?

_____

14. How do they react to Pugnax's cooking?

_____

15. Is the dinner good?

_____

16. What is Pugnax's reward for a job well done?

_____

B) Answer these questions in complete Latin sentences. One or two word answers are not acceptable.

1. Ubi labōrat Pugnax?

_____

2. Estne Pugnax coquus malus?

_____

3. Quid gustat Pugnax?

_____

4. Ubi est Caecilius hodiē?

_____

5. Quis est Titus Claudius Vērus?

_____

6. Salūtatne Claudius Caecilium?

_____

7. Salūtatne Caecilius Calpurniam?

_____

_____

8. Salūtatne Claudius Quintum?

_____

9. Quis vocat Claudium et Caecilium?

_____

10. Ubi cēnant Calpurnia, Caecilius, et Claudius?

_____

11. Estne cēna splendida?

_____

12. Amantne Claudius, Calpurnia, et Caecilius cēnam?

_____

13. Sedetne Pugnax?

_____

14. Estne coquus etiam contentus?

_____

NARRĀTIO

THE ROMAN TABLE

The Romans were expert cooks and had a great appreciation for the preparation (and consumption) of fine food. As the influence of Rome extended further and further from Rome itself and into new and distant lands, Roman legionnaires found themselves exposed to new, exotic foods and customs. Naturally, when they returned to Rome, they brought many of them back with them—often including the foreign cooks themselves! (In the story about the *cēna splendida,* what is Pugnax's nationality?)

Before long, Roman housewives found that they were no longer limited to locally grown products, but instead could choose from a wide variety of imported fruits, vegetables, and meats. As a result, the daily fare of the Roman became more elaborate, varied, and interesting. In fact, during the time of the Empire, entertaining on a lavish scale became quite the fashion for those who could afford it.

A typical table might bear plums from Damascus, lemons and pomegranates from Africa, pepper (especially favored by Roman cooks) and other spices from India and the Far East, and pork from Gaul. Although sugar was known to the Romans, they preferred to use honey as a sweetener in breads and a variety of pastries and tarts. Romans ate their meals at about the same times that we do today. Only the evening meal, however, was a serious eating affair that required a set table.

Ientāculum et Prandium:
A Quick Breakfast and Lunch

Because the Romans were traditionally early risers, ***ientāculum*** (breakfast) was usually eaten very early in the morning, sometimes before dawn. ***Ientāculum*** probably consisted of nothing more than a cup of water, a crust of bread, and from time to time, perhaps a little cheese or fruit. After this simple meal, the family was ready to begin the day's activities.

At about eleven or twelve o'clock, the morning's business affairs were interrupted by ***prandium*** (lunch). Those who had business to conduct in the city could purchase their ***prandium*** in a public eating place. More often than not, however, ***prandium*** was eaten at home. In either case, it was usually a casual meal that was dispensed with rather quickly, much as the ***ientāculum*** was.

Prandium might consist of cold meats, vegetables, fruit, bread, and perhaps a little wine. Romans were particularly fond of wine as a beverage and produced many different kinds from the grapes that grew on the fertile hillsides surrounding the city.

CĒNA: A MEAL FIT FOR A KING

The day's activities continued through the early afternoon until about four o'clock, when everyone attended the public baths to visit, to relax, to see their friends, and to be seen by others (see page CXXVII, The Roman Baths). After returning home, it was time for the last and most important meal of the day, **cēna** or dinner. And what a meal it was, sometimes (for the wealthier Romans) consisting of as many as 15 to 20 different courses and lasting well into the night. On very important occasions, **cēna** would even continue into the next day!

Cēna was the only meal of the day that was served formally in the **triclīnium** or dining room. The name **triclīnium** comes from a type of couch (also called a **triclīnium**) on which diners reclined while eating. Usually, three **triclīnia**—each with space for three people—were grouped around a small, square, cloth-covered table on which food was served. Although not *all* Romans reclined while eating, it was considered a mark of elegance and social distinction.

Children, slaves, and people of the lower classes, as well as travelers at inns, usually ate sitting up. Masters sometimes granted permission to their slaves to eat in a reclining position on special holidays. Diners ate with knives and spoons as well as with their fingers. As a rule, forks were not used in Rome, but toothpicks and large napkins were. In fact, guests often brought their own napkins in which they could carry away uneaten tidbits of meat and vegetables at the conclusion of the meal. It was a custom that was permitted and encouraged. (And you thought that "doggie bags" were a modern invention!)

Between the different courses of the meal, there was entertainment of various sorts—jugglers, dancers, storytelling—and the air was scented with perfumes. Specific fragrances were considered appropriate for specific dishes. There were even specially trained slaves who could explain to any inquiring guest precisely how each dish was prepared, just in case he or she should like to duplicate the fare at home.

History books sometimes portray Romans gorging themselves at elaborate banquets that turned into wild feasts. We know, however, that most Roman meals were likely to be served in elegant and discreet simplicity. The ancient Romans delighted in the proper preparation, seasoning, and presentation of food, and it was generally much appreciated and savored by those who ate it.

II. QUAESTIŌNĒS

Complete the following sentences, which are based on the *Narrātio* about the Roman table.

1. Rome and the Romans were introduced to new and exotic foods because

   _____

   _____

   _____

2. The names of the three meals a Roman ate in a day were _____

   _____

3. Breakfast (_____) usually consisted of _____
               (LATIN NAME)

   _____

4. Lunch (_____) usually consisted of _____
           (LATIN NAME)

   _____

5. Roman table etiquette differed from modern-day table etiquette in the following ways.

   _____

   _____

   _____

6. Did all Romans recline while eating? (Be specific in your answer.)

   _____

   _____

7. Why did Romans bring their own napkins when they were invited to someone else's house for dinner?

   _____

   _____

8. The name of the *Fābula* at the beginning of Chapter XIII is *Pugnax, Familia et Cēna Splendida*. Do you understand now why it was a *splendid* dinner? Do you think that *all* Romans ate 20-course meals on a regular basis? Yes? No? Who did? Who didn't?

III. EXPLICĀTIŌNĒS

THE PRESENT TENSE AND ITS TRANSLATION

Let's take a moment to look at one particular difference between English and Latin that often causes problems for students who want to translate both from Latin to English and especially from English to Latin.

THE PRESENT TENSE DESCRIBES WHAT'S HAPPENING RIGHT NOW!

When we describe an action that is taking place in the present—any action, like *thinking, watching, seeing, laughing*—we are using the *present tense* of the verb. In fact, all of the verbs that you have studied so far in this book have been in the *present tense*. Four of them are listed below.

cōgitō	I think	**rīdeō**	I laugh
spectō	I watch	**videō**	I see

In Latin, there is only **one** way to express the idea that *I* (a person) *am laughing right now at this present time*, and that is with the single word rīdeō.

THE THREE TRANSLATIONS OF "RĪDEŌ" IN ENGLISH

English speakers, however, feel that it is important to make some other distinctions that the Romans did not feel were necessary. In English, we indicate the most general translation of *rīdeō* (meaning that laughing is *generally something that I do*) with these words:

> I laugh   (general statement)

We can also be more precise in our concept of *laughing* by indicating that it is *something that I am in the process of doing right at this moment*. We can say:

> I am laughing   (continuing action)

In addition, we can go even further by *insisting* that it is something of which we are capable:

> I do laugh   (insistence)

Each of these three English expressions above represents an action that is taking place in the present time, but each one puts a little different emphasis on just exactly what is happening in the present time.

SO WHAT'S OUR CONCLUSION?

Where Latin has only **one** way to express present tense, English has **three** ways, each one suggesting a different aspect of present time.

> **rīdeō**   I laugh (general)
> **rīdeō**   I am laughing (continuing)
> **rīdeō**   I do laugh (insistence)

If the Romans studied English, you can imagine the problems they would have. Every time they wanted to express an action in the present—even the most simple of actions—they would have to decide beforehand if it was a *continuing* action, an *insisting* action, or just a *general* statement. In their own language, they were never faced with these decisions because in Latin there was only one way to express an action in the present time.

─────────── IV. EXERCITĀTIŌNĒS ───────────

A)   Translate the verbs in the list below into English. Each Latin verb will have three possible translations in English—general, continuing, insistence.

1.   sedeō

   _____

   _____

   _____

4.   parō

   _____

   _____

   _____

2.   auscultās

   _____

   _____

   _____

5.   respondēmus

   _____

   _____

   _____

3.   terreō

   _____

   _____

   _____

6.   labōrātis

   _____

   _____

   _____

B) Translate these verbs into Latin.

1. he is injuring _____

2. she carries _____

3. he does provide _____

4. we are finishing _____

5. you (*singular*) prepare _____

6. I am answering _____

7. I do wound _____

8. we are crying _____

9. they are entering _____

10. she does think _____

11. he is laughing _____

12. you (*singular*) do frighten _____

C) Look at the two columns of sentences below and fill in the missing words. The sentences in the English column have the same meaning as the corresponding sentences in the Latin column. *Be sure to fill in each blank with something.*

1. They _____ crying.

2. She does _____ the food.

3. We are thinking.

4. You are _____ the teacher.

5. They _____ your friend.

6. We _____ answer.

1. Lacrimant.

2. Cibum gustat.

3. _____ .

4. Magistrum salutātis.

5. Amīcum tuum auscultant.

6. _____

D) Before you translate the following sentences, draw a box around each verb and circle each helping verb. Then translate each sentence into GOOD Latin. You may need to consult the *Index Verbōrum* at the back of the book for some of the vocabulary. Be careful to use normal Latin word order and watch for the correct placement of adjectives and verbs!

1. Yes, the cook does live in the old house and he is working in the kitchen again, today.

   _____

   _____

2. I am watching the good-looking boy by the tree in the garden. He is delightful!

   _____

   _____

3. No, your friend is not visiting the school today. Does he live in Greece?

   _____

   _____

4. Gāius and Tiberius are sitting in the road and laughing! Father is angry.

   _____

   _____

5. They are always praising the teacher. Do they also praise the student?

   _____

   _____

6. The poet loves his dinner; therefore (ergo), he is praising his cook.

   _____

LECTIO XIV

The Latin Connection: Part II

I. EXPLICĀTIŌNĒS

DERIVATIVES REVISITED

In Chapter VIII we looked at a few of the many English words that come to us from Latin. Although these words are often changed in spelling, they usually keep the meaning of the original Latin word and also the spelling of the Latin root. Such English words are called *derivatives*. For example, look at the following words:

ex	port	
im	port	
de	port	
	port	able
	port	er
trans	port	ation

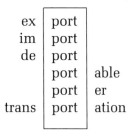

PORTER = PORTO, PORTARE

We already know that the Latin word *portāre* means _____. Each of the words above contains the Latin root port in it, so we can conclude that each of these words has something to do with the idea of *carrying*.

If you cover up the boxed-in portion of the words listed above with your finger, you are left with some extra syllables—some of them appear *before* the Latin root and some appear *after* it.

NOTĀ BENE

The syllables that come *before* the root are **prefixes.**

The syllables that come *after* the root are **suffixes.**

The prefixes and suffixes make a difference in the exact meaning of the English word. Write the four prefixes and three suffixes that appear in the list above in these spaces:

PREFIXES: _____ _____   SUFFIXES: _____ _____

_____ _____   _____

PREFIXES AND SUFFIXES

Here is a short list of some common prefixes and suffixes (and their meanings) that we find on many ordinary English words.

PREFIXES	ENGLISH MEANING	SUFFIXES	ENGLISH MEANING
ab-, a-	= from, away	**-able, -ible**	= able to be
ad-	= to, toward, near	**-al**	= pertaining to
ante-	= before	**-ary, -ory**	= relating to
com-, con-, col-	= with, together	**-ate**	= do, make, cause
de-	= away, down	**-ment**	= condition or quality
ex-, e-	= out of, out from	**-or, -tor, -er**	= one who (does)
in-, im-	= into, in; not	**-ous**	= full of
post-	= after	**-tion, -sion**	= act or state of
pre-	= before		
re-	= again or back		
sub-, sup-	= under, below		
trans-	= across, through		

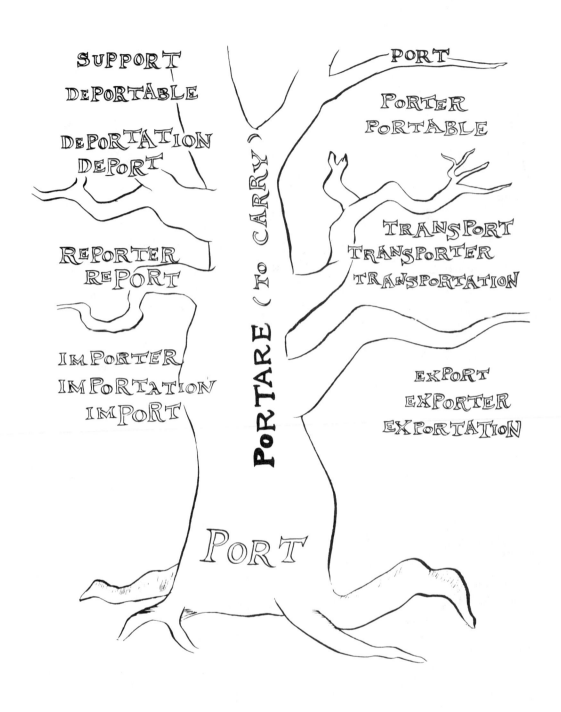

SUPPORT
DEPORTABLE
DEPORTATION
DEPORT

PORT
PORTER
PORTABLE

REPORTER
REPORT

TRANSPORT
TRANSPORTER
TRANSPORTATION

IMPORTER
IMPORTATION
IMPORT

EXPORT
EXPORTER
EXPORTATION

PORTARE (TO CARRY)

PORT

II. EXERCITĀTIŌNĒS

A) Take a look at the derivative tree above. Each of the words on the tree is composed of the Latin root word **port** plus some prefixes and/or suffixes. Use the list on page CCV to separate the words on the next page into their different parts. Be careful! Sometimes a suffix will be preceded by an extra vowel. If you've done the exercise correctly, when you've finished, the sum of all the parts will equal the whole word. **Make sure you check to be sure that this is so.** Look at the example.

	PREFIX	+	ROOT	+	SUFFIX	=	SUM OF THE PARTS
Importation:	IM	+	PORT	+	ATION	=	IMPORTATION
1. Portable:	_____		_____		_____		_____
2. Deportable:	_____		_____		_____		_____
3. Transportation:	_____		_____		_____		_____
4. Importer:	_____		_____		_____		_____
5. Transporter:	_____		_____		_____		_____
6. Import:	_____		_____		_____		_____
7. Porter:	_____		_____		_____		_____
8. Support:	_____		_____		_____		_____
9. Report:	_____		_____		_____		_____
10. Reporter:	_____		_____		_____		_____
11. Deportation:	_____		_____		_____		_____
12. Exporter:	_____		_____		_____		_____

B) Now that you know how to look at a word in order to see its different parts, let's take one more step to discover how the meaning of the original Latin root word is changed by attaching the various suffixes and prefixes to it. If necessary, check the meaning of each prefix or suffix on page CCV to complete the next exercise.

DIRECTIONS: On the next page you will find some of the words from the *portāre* derivative tree. Each word is already broken down for you into its component parts. First, define each part according to what you know about the meaning of the root, prefix, and suffix. Then, use that knowledge to fill in the blanks of each sentence with an appropriate answer. You're going to have to use your head in this exercise. **Make sure that your final English sentence reads correctly.** Check the example.

THE WORD	COMPONENTS	MEANING
IMPORT	a) im =	in, into
	b) port =	carry

c) When we say that we ***import*** televisions from Japan, we really mean that they

are ____carried into____ our country from Japan.

The Word	Components	Meaning

1. PORTABLE   a) port = _____

                b) able = _____

                c) A **portable** television is one that is _____ easily.

2. TRANSPORTATION   a) trans = _____

                b) port = _____

                c) ation = _____

                d) Companies engaged in interstate **transportation** are usually engaged in the _____ of _____ goods _____ state borders.

3. EXPORT   a) ex = _____

                b) port = _____

                c) When we say that we **export** merchandise, we are really saying that we _____ it _____the country.

4. REPORTER   a) re = _____

                b) port = _____

                c) er = _____

                d) A **reporter** is _____ the news _____ to the people.

5. IMPORTATION   a) im = _____

                b) port = _____

                c) ation = _____

                d) The **importation** of foreign automobiles is the _____ of _____ automobiles _____ the country.

THE WORD	COMPONENTS	MEANING

6. IMPORTER   a) <u>im</u> = _____

                         b) <u>port</u> = _____

                         c) <u>er</u> = _____

     d) The **importer** of foreign automobiles is the _____ automobiles

            _____ the country.

7. Circle the appropriate answers below.
     a) The suffix <u>-er</u> on *importer* tells us that this word refers to
         1) a person   2) an action

     b) The suffix <u>-tion</u> on **importation** tells us that this word refers to
         1) a person   2) an action

8. Are you getting the idea now of how a little knowledge about prefixes, suffixes, and roots can give us lots and lots of information about what words mean? How about giving a definition of the following words based on the model of answers 1 through 7 of this exercise?

     What do the following words mean?

     a)   Porter: _____

     b)   Transport: _____

     c)   Exportation: _____

     d)   Deportation: _____

     e)   Exporter: _____

     f)   Supporter: _____

     g)   Report: _____

     h)   Deport: _____

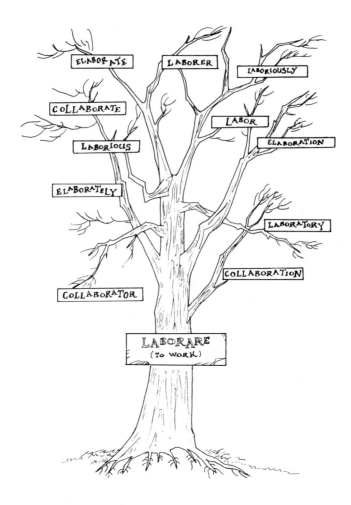

C) Look at the *labōrāre* derivative tree, then do the exercise. Be sure to follow the directions carefully.

DIRECTIONS: Listed below are some of the words from the *labōrāre* derivative tree.

1. Break down each word into its component parts (prefix, root, suffix).
2. In the space below each component, write in the meaning of that particular component, checking the prefix/ suffix list if needed.
3. Finally, fill in the blanks in the sentence using what you have learned about the meaning of the word.
4. Make sure that your final sentence is a CORRECT English sentence.

		PREFIX	ROOT	SUFFIX
IMPORT	a)	im	port	—
	b)	in, into	carry	—

c) ***Importing*** goods means that we ___carry them into___ the country.

NŌMEN_____

DIĒS_____

	Prefix	Root	Suffix

1. LABORER   a) _____   _____   _____

           b) _____   _____   _____

   c) A **laborer** is _____.

2. LABORATORY   a) _____   _____   _____

           b) _____   _____   _____

   c) A **laboratory** is a place _____.

3. LABORIOUS   a) _____   _____   _____

           b) _____   _____   _____

   c) A **laborious** task is one that is _____.

4. ELABORATE   a) _____   _____   _____

           b) _____   _____   _____

   c) When we **elaborate** on a subject, what we really do is _____

     _____.

5. COLLABORATOR   a) _____   _____   _____

           b) _____   _____   _____

   c) A **collaborator** on a book is _____ another person to produce a book.

6. COLLABORATE   a) _____   _____   _____

           b) _____   _____   _____

   c) When two crooks plan together to rob a bank, we say that they **collaborate** to rob the bank; that is, they _____.

7. COLLABORATION   a) _____   _____   _____

           b) _____   _____   _____

   c) The **collaboration** of two or more people on any project means that they are engaged in _____ to obtain certain desired results.

D) Here is another exercise similar to Exercise C, except that in this exercise, there are words based on many *different* Latin roots. All of them are ordinary English words in current usage. Some of them you may know, others you may not. Before you break down the word into its component parts, first, choose the Latin word (from the list given) from which the English word is derived and write it in blank (a). Then follow the same directions as for Exercise C.

rīdēre	vocāre	cōgitāre	terrēre
auscultāre	laudāre	tenēre	movēre

English Word	Prefix	Root	Suffix
IMMOVABLE	a) movēre		
	b) im	mov	able
	c) not	move	able to be

d)   An ***immovable*** object is one which is ___not able to be moved___.

1.   LAUDABLE   a) _____

b) _____   _____   _____

c) _____   _____   _____

d)   If we say that someone made a ***laudable*** speech, we mean it is a speech

that _____.

2.   REVOCATION   a) _____

b) _____   _____   _____

c) _____   _____   _____

d)   They had to close the business because their license was ***revoked.***

Revocation of a license means _____ a license by the state or other regulatory agency.

3.   DETER   a) _____

b) _____   _____   _____

c) _____   _____   _____

d)   When we say that the threat of punishment ***deters*** criminals from

committing more crimes, we really mean that punishment _____

them _____ _____ committing more crimes.

English Word	Prefix	Root	Suffix

4. DERIDE a) _____

  b) _____ _____ _____

  c) _____ _____ _____

  d) Teachers who **deride** their students' efforts to improve are not very good teachers because that means that they _____ at the students contemptuously.

5. CONVOCATION a) _____

  b) _____ _____ _____

  c) _____ _____ _____

  d) A **convocation** of business people is _____

  _____.

6. COGITATION a) _____

  b) _____ _____ _____

  c) _____ _____ _____

  d) **Cogitation** means _____.

7. AMATORY a) _____

  b) _____ _____ _____

  c) _____ _____ _____

  d) **Amatory** means _____.

8. TERRIBLE a) _____

  b) _____ _____ _____

  c) _____ _____ _____

  d) According to what you know about Latin and what you discovered above, state here what the expression **a terrible house** ORIGINALLY meant in English.

  _____

In modern English, however, the word *terrible* has taken on a much lighter meaning than it originally had. For example, if I told you that I moved out of a *terrible* house last week, you would understand that (circle one)

> **1.** the house was haunted.
> **2.** the house was in bad condition.

Now, consult a dictionary to verify the meaning of *terrible*. You should find *both* of the meanings of the word. Copy the parts of the definition from the dictionary that cover both senses of the word in the spaces provided below.

LITERAL MEANING: TERRIBLE HOUSE (TERRIFYING, SUCH AS HAUNTED)

_____

_____

_____

MODERN MEANING: TERRIBLE HOUSE (POOR CONDITION)

_____

_____

_____

E) END-TO-END WORD SEARCH: The word search on the next page is composed of English words arranged end to end. Every letter counts. There are NO letters left over. If you read each line from left to right and you do not skip any lines, you will read all of the words on the maze. Be careful! Some words do not fit completely on one line and are continued on the next. There are 18 English words in the maze. They are all words that have been derived from the Latin verbs that you have been studying in Chapters XI, XII, and XIII. Can you *make the Latin connection?*

DIRECTIONS: As you read off each word, decide from which Latin verb it is derived and then write both principal parts of the verb (*first person singular* and *infinitive*) and the meaning of the infinitive form on the answer sheet on the next page. Below this information, write each word you encounter in the maze that is derived from the **same** Latin verb. When you finish, you will have *six* different Latin root words and under each one, you will have from one to five derivatives for a total of 18 derivative words. Good luck!

NŌMEN _____

DIĒS _____

END-TO-END WORD SEARCH

T	E	R	R	O	R	I	Z	E	D	E	T	E	R
R	E	D	D	E	R	I	D	E	P	R	O	V	O
C	A	T	I	O	N	S	E	D	A	T	I	O	N
C	O	L	L	A	B	O	R	A	T	I	V	E	B
E	L	A	B	O	R	R	I	D	I	C	U	L	O
U	S	T	E	R	R	I	F	Y	C	O	G	I	T
A	T	O	R	V	O	C	A	T	I	O	N	L	A
B	O	R	I	O	U	S	L	Y	T	E	R	R	I
F	I	C	R	I	D	I	C	U	L	E	D	C	O
N	V	O	K	E	P	R	O	V	O	K	E	D	I
N	V	O	K	I	N	G	L	A	B	O	R	E	R

END-TO-END WORD SEARCH: ANSWER SHEET

1. a) Latin verb (root):

    _____

    _____

    b) English meaning:

    _____

    c) English derivatives:

    _____

    _____

    _____

    _____

2. a) Latin verb (root):

    _____

    _____

    b) English meaning:

    _____

    c) English derivatives:

    _____

    _____

    _____

    _____

3. a) Latin verb (root):

    _____

    _____

    b) English meaning:

    _____

    c) English derivatives:

    _____

    _____

    _____

    _____

4. a) Latin verb (root):

    _____

    _____

    b) English meaning:

    _____

    c) English derivatives:

    _____

    _____

    _____

    _____

5. a) Latin verb (root):

    _____

    _____

    b) English meaning:

    _____

    c) English derivatives:

    _____

    _____

    _____

6. a) Latin verb (root):

    _____

    _____

    b) English meaning:

    _____

    c) English derivatives:

    _____

    _____

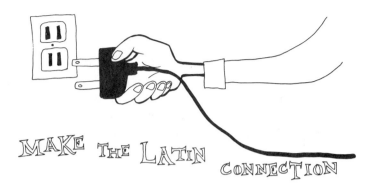

A Final Look at How Derivatives Come into Our Language from Latin

The Four Principal Parts of a Latin Verb

In the preceding chapters we learned that a Latin dictionary lists verbs according to their *first person singular* forms and that the *infinitive* form of a verb is also given.

pulsō, pulsāre = to hit
sedeō, sedēre = to sit

Along with the first person singular form and the infinitive, a dictionary usually lists *two other verb forms*. The two verbs that we listed above would look like this in the dictionary:

pulsō, pulsāre, pulsāvī, pulsātus = to hit
sedeō, sedēre, sedī, sessus = to sit

These are called the **four principal parts** of a verb. All regular Latin verbs have four principal parts that together give us all the information we need in order to use the word correctly in any possible situation.

In this book, we will concentrate our efforts on the *fourth principal part* of the verbs we have already studied, and leave the study of the third principal part for another time. All verbs presented in the text from now on will include the *first, second,* and *fourth* principal parts (*pulsō, pulsāre, pulsātus*). In the *Index Verbōrum* at the back of the book, all verbs are listed this way.

Notā Bene

The third and fourth principal parts of a verb are *additional* forms. They are not part of the regular conjugation of the verbs that we have learned and they do *not* influence in any way the conjugation of the present tense verbs that we have learned.

There is an advantage to learning the fourth principal parts of all of the verbs we've studied because they help us become aware of many more derivatives.

Take the verb *sedeō*, for instance. If you did not know the different principal parts of that verb, it would be much more difficult to see that the two English words *sediment* and *session* are *both* related to the *same* Latin root word that means *to sit*. *Sediment* is derived from the infinitive form (*sedēre*) of the verb *sedeō*, and *session* comes from the fourth principal part (*sessus*) of the same verb. Both *sediment* and *session* have something to do with *sitting*.

Sediment is the material that collects or "sits" on the bottom of a riverbed at the mouth of a river.

A *session* of the state legislature is the period in which the legislators "sit" in meeting.

It would be a lot harder to see the connection of both of these English words to the Latin verb *sedēre* (and to each other) if we didn't know that fourth principal part.

GLADIATORS—ROME'S ROCK STARS!

The word "gladiator" is based on the Latin word, *gladius* (sword). In early Roman times, these specialized "sword bearers" were criminals, slaves, or prisoners who were forced to fight to the death before large audiences. Special schools were founded for training gladiators. Contenders could earn their freedom after a certain number of bouts or years of service. Successful gladiators earned popular reputations and were admired by their fans, much as our rock stars are today. In later Roman times, freedmen, knights, and even senators and women entered the gladitorial arena for pay or glory. It was by far the most popular spectator sport of the day and finally reached such outrageous proportions that the Emperor Augustus was forced to put limits on the number and types of combat.

F) Look at the four groups of words below. Each contains a Latin verb (infinitive and fourth principal part) plus some common English derivatives. The stems of all of the Latin verbs have already been underlined.

    Your job is to underline the part of each English word that contains one of the stems, then make the connection between the English words and the correct principal part of its verbal ancestor. Did the English derivative come from a) the *infinitive* form of the verb or b) the *fourth principal part* of the verb? Indicate your answer by writing the correct form of the verb in the blank next to each derivative.

1.   TO SEE: a)   vidē/re

               b)   vīs/us

vidēre	videotape
vīsus	television
_____	visionary
_____	improvident
_____	improvise
_____	evidently

2.   TO LIVE: a)   habitā/re

               b)   habitāt/us

_____	inhabit
_____	habitat
_____	habitation
_____	co-habit
_____	co-habitation
_____	habitable

3.   TO WORK: a)   labōrā/re

               b)   labōrāt/us

_____	belabor
_____	laboratory
_____	collaboration
_____	laboriously
_____	elaborating
_____	labored

4.   TO END: a)   terminā/re

               b)   terminat/us

_____	terminal
_____	terminator
_____	interminable
_____	determine
_____	extermination
_____	terminative

G) Here is an alphabetical listing of all the verbs we studied in Chapters XI, XII, and XIII. In the blanks on the left, indicate to which conjugation each verb belongs (*first* or *second*) and then use this list to help you do the exercise in Part I.

_____   **1.**   ambulō, ambulāre, ambulātus   to walk

_____   **2.**   amō, amāre, amātus   to love, to like

_____	3.	auscultō, auscultāre, auscultātus	to listen (to)
_____	4.	cēnō, cēnāre, cēnātus	to dine, have dinner
_____	5.	clāmō, clāmāre, clāmātus	to call, shout
_____	6.	cōgitō, cōgitāre, cōgitātus	to think
_____	7.	gustō, gustāre, gustātus	to taste
_____	8.	habeō, habēre, habitus	to have
_____	9.	habitō, habitāre, habitātus	to live
_____	10.	intrō, intrāre, intrātus	to enter, walk into
_____	11.	labōrō, labōrāre, labōrātus	to work, toil
_____	12.	lacrimō, lacrimāre, lacrimātus	to cry, weep
_____	13.	laudō, laudāre, laudātus	to praise
_____	14.	locō, locāre, locātus	to place, to put
_____	15.	moneō, monēre, monītus	to warn, advise
_____	16.	moveō, movēre, mōtus	to move
_____	17.	narrō, narrāre, narrātus	to relate, tell
_____	18.	parō, parāre, parātus	to prepare
_____	19.	portō, portāre, portātus	to carry
_____	20.	prōvideō, prōvidēre, prōvīsus	to provide, foresee
_____	21.	pugnō, pugnāre, pugnātus	to fight
_____	22.	pulsō, pulsāre, pulsātus	to strike, hit
_____	23.	respondeō, respondēre, respōnsus	to reply, answer
_____	24.	rīdeō, rīdēre, rīsus	to laugh, smile
_____	25.	salūtō, salūtāre, salūtātus	to greet
_____	26.	sedeō, sedēre, sessus	to sit
_____	27.	spectō, spectāre, spectātus	to look at, watch
_____	28.	teneō, tenēre, tentus	to hold
_____	29.	terminō, termināre, terminātus	to end, finish
_____	30.	terreō, terrēre, territus	to frighten

_____	**31.** videō, vidēre, vīsus	to see
_____	**32.** vīsitō, vīsitāre, vīsitātus	to visit
_____	**33.** vocō, vocāre, vocātus	to call, invite
_____	**34.** vulnerō, vulnerāre, vulnerātus	to wound

NOTĀ BENE

What are the last four letters of the fourth principal parts of each **first conjugation verb** on the list in Part H?

_____

The formation of the fourth principal part for all **first conjugation** verbs is *regular*. That is, it follows the same pattern every time.

The formation of the fourth principal part for **second conjugation** verbs is *irregular*. That is, it does not always follow the same pattern for every verb.

H) Each of the pairs of English words listed below is derived from different principal parts of the same Latin verb. Write the correct principal part (infinitive or fourth principal part) of the Latin verb from which the English word is derived. Use the verb list on pages CCXIX–CCXXI as a guide.

	labōrāre	laboriously	**4.**	_____	response
	labōrātus	laboratory		_____	responding
1.	_____	provide	**5.**	_____	movement
	_____	provisions		_____	motorized
2.	_____	vocation	**6.**	_____	amble
	_____	vocal		_____	ambulatory
3.	_____	intersession	**7.**	_____	narrate
	_____	sedentary		_____	narrative

NŌMEN _____

DIĒS _____

I) Use the directions below for both the exercise that follows and the exercise in Part **J.** In these exercises the words are not arranged in pairs and you may not know the meaning of all of them. Nevertheless, your knowledge of Latin will allow you to make some intelligent guesses as to what they may mean. See how many you can answer correctly without using the dictionary.

DIRECTIONS:
a) First, decide which Latin verb on pages CCXIX–CCXXI most closely resembles the word given. Write the *first person singular* form of that verb in blank *a*.

b) In blank *b* write the specific principal part from which the English word is derived (*infinitive* or *fourth principal part*).

c) In blank *c* write the English infinitive form of the Latin verb.

d) Finally, complete the sentence to make a true statement. Follow the example.

HINT: If you get stuck on a word, it is helpful to remember what we learned about prefixes and suffixes (pages CCV–CCXII). By subtracting the prefixes and suffixes from a word, it is much easier to see the stem or root.

PROBABLY COMES FROM THE VERB	CORRECT PRINCIPAL PART	WHICH MEANS (IN ENGLISH)

DERIDE

a) ___rīdeō___   b) ___rīdēre___   c) ___to laugh___

d) Therefore the English word ___deride___ has something to do with ___laughing___.

1. LAUD

a) _____   b) _____   c) _____

d) Therefore the English word _____ has something to do with _____.

2. AMBULANT

a) _____   b) _____   c) _____

d) Therefore the English word _____ has something to do with _____.

	PROBABLY COMES FROM THE VERB	CORRECT PRINCIPAL PART	WHICH MEANS (IN ENGLISH)

3. DERISIVE

   a) _____ b) _____ c) _____

   d) Therefore the English word _____ has something to do with

   _____.

4. TERRIFY

   a) _____ b) _____ c) _____

   d) Therefore the English word _____ has something to do with

   _____.

5. SALUTE

   a) _____ b) _____ c) _____

   d) Therefore the English word _____ has something to do with

   _____.

6. AMATEUR

   a) _____ b) _____ c) _____

   d) Therefore the English word _____ has something to do with

   _____.

7. LACRIMATION

   a) _____ b) _____ c) _____

   d) Therefore the English word _____ has something to do

   with _____.

8. AUSCULTATORY

   a) _____ b) _____ c) _____

   d) Therefore the English word _____ has something to do

   with _____.

> ## CREATIVE DERIVATION: A COMPETITIVE SPORT
>
> Class members group into pairs.
>
> Using the Latin vocabulary you have studied to this point, see how many NEW English words you can create **THAT DO NOT EXIST IN THE ENGLISH LANGUAGE BUT COULD OR SHOULD.** Be sure to give a proper definition to your made-up word, its Latin roots and a sentence that illustrates its proper use.
>
> **AN EXAMPLE:** *Abtenate: to hold away (from oneself)*
> (Latin: *ab + tenēo, tenēre*)
> John *abtenated* the poor poodle who had been attacked by the skunk.
>
> The group with the largest number of viable creations wins the competition.
>
> To test the validity of your entries, read your sentences aloud and have the class guess at their meanings and give the Latin root words from which they are derived.

J) See the directions for Part I.

	PROBABLY COMES FROM THE VERB	CORRECT PRINCIPAL PART	WHICH MEANS (IN ENGLISH)

1.   COGITATION

a) _____   b) _____   c) _____

d) Therefore the English word _____ has something to do with _____.

2.   MOTIVATED

a) _____   b) _____   c) _____

d) Therefore the English word _____ has something to do with _____.

PROBABLY COMES FROM THE VERB	CORRECT PRINCIPAL PART	WHICH MEANS (IN ENGLISH)

3. SALUTATION

    a) _____   b) _____   c) _____

    d) Therefore the English word _____ has something to do with _____.

4. RESPONSIVE

    a) _____   b) _____   c) _____

    d) Therefore the English word _____ has something to do with _____.

5. PULSATION

    a) _____   b) _____   c) _____

    d) Therefore the English word _____ has something to do with _____.

6. MOVIES

    a) _____   b) _____   c) _____

    d) Therefore the English word _____ has something to do with _____.

7. RIDICULOUS

    a) _____   b) _____   c) _____

    d) Therefore the English word _____ has something to do with _____.

8. LAUDATORY

    a) _____   b) _____   c) _____

    d) Therefore the English word _____ has something to do with _____.

LECTIO XV

Playing the Plurals Game

THE
ROMAN EMPIRE
117 A.D.

Read the following Latin story. Some of the vocabulary words are given to you in the *Index Verbōrum* on the next page, but not all of them. Use your "Latin intuition" to figure out the others.

HISTORIA: IMPERIUM RŌMĀNUM

Rōma in Ītaliā est. Ītalia paeninsula est. Graecia paeninsula etiam est. Graecia in trēs partēs dīvīsa est: Macedonia, Epīrus, et Achāia. Ītalia, Graecia, et Hispānia in Eurōpā sunt.

Estne Britannia paeninsula? Minimē, nōn est. Britannia magna insula est. Sicilia et Crēta quoque insulae magnae sunt. Sicilia et Crēta in Marī Internō sunt sed Britannia in Marī Internō nōn est.

In Galliā, Iūlius Caesar pugnat. Victoriae suae sunt magnae. Caesar Britanniam etiam videt et ad magnam insulam nāvigat. Nunc Caesar magnam glōriam habet et Imperium Rōmānum magnum est.

Ītalia, Graecia, Hispānia, Gallia, et Britannia in Eurōpā sunt. Estne etiam Aegyptus in Eurōpā? Minimē, Aegyptus in Eurōpā nōn est. Aegyptus in Africā est. Imperium Rōmānum est in Eurōpā, in Africā, et in Asiā. Imperium Rōmānum est maximum.

INDEX VERBŌRUM

ad (+ accusative) to, towards
dīvīsus, dīvīsa divided
Gallia France
glōria glory, fame
quoque also
imperium empire (neuter)
Marī Internō ablative of Mare Internum

maximus, maxima biggest, very big
nāvigō, nāvigāre, nāvigātus to sail
pugnō, pugnāre, pugnātus to fight

NOTĀ BENE

Imperium is a neuter noun. Its nominative case ending is **-um**.

Marī Internō is the ablative case of *Mare Internum*. Use your "Latin intuition" to figure out what it is.

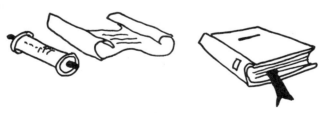

Librī sunt.

I. ANALYSIS EXERCISE

ANALYSIS QUESTION
What do we know about the Roman Empire?

1. The narrative indicates that *Ītalia* is a *paeninsula* and that *Britannia* is an *insula*. What are the English equivalents of these two words? Be careful of spelling.

    paeninsula = _____

    insula   = _____

2. Knowing what you do about the Latin word *insula*, can you explain in your own words how it led to our English words *insulate/insulation*? (*What do we do when we insulate a house?*)

    _____

    _____

    _____

3. Macedonia was an ancient kingdom that was eventually absorbed by the growing Roman Empire. Look in the gazeteer section of a dictionary (you may have to go to the library if your dictionary does not have a gazeteer section) to find out what modern-day countries (or sections of countries) were carved out of the ancient kingdom of Macedonia. Write your answers on the line below.

_____

4. Compare the map on page CCXXVI with the one facing page I, then answer the following questions.

   a) What was the Roman name for modern-day France?

   _____

   b) Paris is the capital of France today. By what name was it known to the Romans?

   _____

   c) What modern-day country did *Hispānia* become?

   _____

   d) What modern-day country did *Dācia* become?

   _____

   e) What modern-day country did *Thrācē* become?

   _____

5. a) On what continent is *Ītalia?* _____

   b) On what continent is *Aegyptus?* _____

   c) On what continent is *Armenia?* _____

6. Looking at the map on page CCXXVI, what do you think *mare* means in English?

   _____

7. Using your "Latin intuition" and what you know about derivatives, what do you think *internum* means?

    _____

8. Can you state in your own words why the Mediterranean Sea was called *Mare Internum* by the Romans?

    _____

    _____

9. The Mediterranean Sea was also known in Rome as *Mare Nostrum*. Can you also explain why the Romans called it that?

    _____

    _____

II. ANALYSIS EXERCISE

ANALYSIS QUESTION

How do we form the plural in Latin?

APPIAN WAY

THE APPIAN WAY—SUPER HIGHWAY OF THE ROMAN EMPIRE

The *Via Appia* is the oldest of the many excellent Roman roadways that connected the cities and towns of the Roman Empire together. Begun in 312 B.C. and known as the "Queen of Roads," the initial leg of the famous highway linked Rome to Capua, 132 miles away. It was later extended to Brindisium, 234 miles from Rome. The *Via Appia*, however, was only the first leg of a 50,000-mile network of highways that eventually extended throughout the entire Roman Empire, covering what would become 30 separate, modern-day nations.

Although an efficient highway system facilitated the exchange of people, ideas, styles, and goods among the various parts of the Empire (and contributed greatly to its unity), the real purpose of the highway network was mainly military. It was much easier for Rome to administer and maintain control of far-away conquered lands if Roman legions could be guaranteed relatively easy access.

The Romans were so successful at building roads that many parts of the original highway network were still in use during the Middle Ages. Even today, more than 2,000 years later, some stretches of the Appian Way are still in existence.

AN EXERCISE IN PLURALITY

1. Write the first sentence of the Historia on page CCXXVII on line *a* below. Then write the third sentence of the *Historia* on line *b*. Finally, on line *c*, write the last line of the first paragraph. When you have finished, translate each sentence into GOOD English on the lines provided.

   a) _____
   _____

   b) _____
   _____

   c) _____
   _____

2. Now compare the three Latin sentences that you have written. Each sentence is composed of a subject, a verb, and some other words. Write the single Latin word that is the subject of sentence *a* on line *a* in the space provided following this paragraph. Then write the single Latin word that is the subject of sentence *b* on line *b*, and *the complete subject* of sentence *c* on line *c*. Indicate in the blank on the left if the subject is singular or plural (S or P).

   _____ a) _____
   _____ b) _____
   _____ c) _____

Romānī sunt.

Notā Bene

Complete the blanks below on the basis of what you have done so far in this Analysis Exercise.

The word *est* is a Latin verb. It is _____ and it means
(SINGULAR/PLURAL)

_____ in English. When *est* is the verb of the sentence, the subject

is _____ .
(SINGULAR/PLURAL)

The word *sunt* is also a Latin verb. It is _____ and it means
(SINGULAR/PLURAL)

_____ in English. When *sunt* is the verb of the sentence, the subject

is _____ .
(SINGULAR/PLURAL)

Conclusion

There _____ agreement in the *number* of the subject and its verb.
(IS/IS NOT)

---

3. Look at the three sentences below:

   a) Sicilia est insula magna.
   b) Crēta est insula magna.
   c) Sicilia et Crēta sunt insulae magnae.

4. Translate the three sentences above into GOOD English. Use your common sense for the last sentence.

   a) _____

   b) _____

   c) _____

5. Analyze the words *insula* and *insulae* by filling in the blanks below:

	CASE	GENDER	NUMBER
insula	——————————	——————————	——————————
insulae	——————————	——————————	——————————

CONCLUSIONS

THE PLURAL OF FIRST DECLENSION NOUNS

The plural of *insula* is ——————————————————————.

The ending **-ae** is the plural form of what feminine singular *Latin* ending?

——————

The ending **-ae** corresponds to what *English* plural ending? ——————————

---

6. Look at these two sentences.

   a) Trānio est servus Rōmānus.
   b) Clēmens est servus Rōmānus.

   Now, turn to page LXXVIII and complete the last caption.

   c) Trānio et Clēmens ————————————————————

7. Translate the three sentences above into GOOD English.

   a) ————————————————————————————

   b) ————————————————————————————

   c) ————————————————————————————

8. Analyze the words *servus* and *servī*.

	CASE	GENDER	NUMBER
servus	_____	_____	_____
servī	_____	_____	_____

CONCLUSIONS

THE PLURAL OF SECOND DECLENSION NOUNS

The plural of the noun *servus* is _____ .

The ending **-ī** is the plural form of what masculine singular *Latin* ending?

_____

The ending **-ī** corresponds to what *English* plural ending? _____

---

9. Circle the correct responses for the following questions.

a) Looking back at the third and sixth questions of this Analysis Exercise, the words *magna* and *Rōmānus* are

    nouns   adjectives   verbs   other

b) When *insula* is plural, *magna* is plural.

The plural form of *magna* is _____ .

c) When *servus* is plural, *Rōmānus* is plural, also.

The plural form of Rōmānus is _____ .

10. With the above information, we can formulate a new rule:

THE PLURAL ENDINGS OF THE NOMINATIVE CASE

FIRST AND SECOND DECLENSION NOMINATIVE CASE ENDINGS

		Singular		Plural	
First Declension	Feminine	a	becomes	ae
Second Declension	Masculine	us	becomes	ī
Second Declension	Masculine	er	becomes	rī

SOME EXAMPLES

In the plural:	puella	becomes	puell**ae** (girls)
	cathedra	becomes	cathedr**ae** (chairs)
	Rōmānus	becomes	Rōmanī (boys)
	fluvius	becomes	fluviī (rivers)
	magister	becomes	magist**rī** (teachers)
	liber	becomes	librī (books)

Rānae contentae sunt.

NOTĀ BENE: AN EXCEPTION TO THE RULE

The plural of *puer* is irregular and does not follow the rule. The plural of *puer* is *puerī*. It does *not* drop the *e* like *magister* and *liber* (*magistrī* and *librī*).

puer   becomes   *puerī* (boys)

---

11. Look at the following example sentences in both their singular and plural forms, then do the exercises that follow. Complete the fourth sentence with the word *boy* or *boys* in its correct Latin form.

   a) Porta est magna.
      Portae sunt magnae.

   a) The door is big.
      The doors are big.

   b) Equus parātus est.
      Equī parātī sunt.

   b) The horse is ready.
      The horses are ready.

   c) Liber est optimus.
      Librī sunt optimī.

   c) The book is excellent.
      The books are excellent.

   d) _____ formōsus est.

      _____ formōsī sunt.

   d) The boy is handsome.

      The boys are handsome.

Puer est formōsus.

Puerī sunt formōsī.

III. EXERCITĀTIŌNĒS

A) Change the following singular sentences into plural sentences. Then translate each plural sentence into GOOD English. Make sure that your verb is also plural. Consult the vocabulary lists at the back of the book for help with the translations.

1. Tunica est antīqua.

   _____

   _____

2. Lectus est optimus.

   _____

   _____

3. Lūna est magna.

   _____

   _____

4. Pūpa ūmida est.

   _____

   _____

5. Sciūrus est magnus et fuscus.

   _____

   _____

6. Plūma parva est. Longa nōn est.

   _____

   _____

7. Magister tranquillus est.

   _____

   _____

8. Parāta est puella et fīdus est servus.

_____

_____

9. Liber novus et splendidus est.

_____

_____

10. Puer timidus est.

_____

_____

B) *Est* or *sunt?* Which verb is needed in the following sentences, the singular *est* or the plural *sunt?* Write the correct answer in the blank, then translate the sentences into GOOD English.

1. Ubi _____ fenestrae?

_____

2. Ubi _____ paeninsula?

_____

3. Pūpae suae _____ formōsae.

_____

4. _____ ne Britannia magna?

_____

5. Discipulī Rōmānī _____ īrātī.

_____

6. Quis _____ Gāius Iūlius Caesar?

_____

7. Coquī Graecī contentī nōn _____ .

_____

8. Magister in Achāiā hodiē _____ .

_____

9. _____ ne rānae parvae?

_____

10. Ubi _____ amīcī meī?

_____

11. Marcus et Marcellus in hortō _____ .

_____

C) Supply the proper endings (*nominative singular* or *nominative plural*) to the nouns in the following sentences, then translate each sentence into GOOD English.

1. Ubi sunt port_____?

_____

2. Estne papȳr_____ alb_____?

_____

3. Minimē, puell_____ parv_____ in Graeciā nōn sunt.

_____

4. Puer_____ Rōmān_____ rānam parvam vident.

_____

5. Ubi est lib_____ me_____?

_____

6. Suntne fenestr_____ magn_____?

_____

D) *Circle* the subject of each sentence below and *underline* all of the adjectives that describe it. Then rewrite the Latin sentence, making the subject and its adjectives plural. Be careful to make the verb plural, too. Then, translate your new sentence into GOOD English.

1. Coquus stultus iterum nōn est laetus.

   _____

   _____

2. Grammaticus occupātus in Graeciā est.

   _____

   _____

3. Estne puer validus?

   _____

   _____

4. Minimē, fēmina formōsa fatīgāta hodiē nōn est.

   _____

   _____

5. Ita vērō, agricola Rōmānus prope vīllam semper est.

   _____

   _____

6. Estne victōria sua magna?

   _____

   _____

Puellae rīdent.

THE PLURAL ENDINGS OF THE ACCUSATIVE CASE

FIRST AND SECOND DECLENSION
ACCUSATIVE CASE ENDINGS

		Singular		Plural	
First Declension	Feminine	**am**	becomes	**ās**	
Second Declension	Masculine	**um**	becomes	**ōs**	
Second Declension	Masculine	**rum**	becomes	**rōs**	

SOME EXAMPLES

In the plural:	puell**am**	becomes	puell**ās** (girls)
	cathēdr**am**	becomes	cathēdr**as** (chairs)
	Rōmān**um**	becomes	Rōmān**ōs** (boys)
	fluvi**um**	becomes	fluvi**ōs** (rivers)
	magist**rum**	becomes	magist**ros** (teachers)

Gallōs videō.

> ## RULE
>
> **The subject** of a sentence and the verb of a sentence must *agree in number*.
>
> When the **subject** of a sentence becomes plural, the verb also becomes plural.
>
> When the **direct object** of a sentence becomes plural, the verb is unaffected.
>
> **Here are some examples:**
>
> ### Singular and Plural Subjects
>
> 1. Puer est magnus.
>   Puerī sunt magnī.
>
> 1. The boy is big.
>   The boys are big.
>
> 2. Puella puerum videt.
>   Puellae puerum vident.
>
> 2. The girl sees the boy.
>   The girls see the boy.
>
> ### Singular and Plural Direct Objects
>
> 1. Puer taurum videt.
>   Puer taurōs videt.
>
> 1. The boy sees the bull.
>   The boy sees the bulls.

E) Look at the following example sentences in both their singular and plural forms; then do the following exercises.

1. Portam videō.
   Portās videō.

1. I see the door.
   I see the doors.

2. Claudia murum magnum videt.
   Claudia murōs magnōs videt.

2. Claudia sees the big wall.
   Claudia sees the big walls.

3. Puer librum optimum tenet.
   Puer librōs optimōs tenet.

3. The boy holds the excellent book.
   The boy holds the excellent books.

Cathēdrās habeō.   Sellās habeō.

_____ IV. EXERCITĀTIŌNĒS _____

A) In the following sentences, first underline the direct object and any adjectives that accompany it. Then change the direct object (and its adjectives) to its plural form, leaving the rest of the sentence singular. Write the entire sentence in Latin. Finally, translate the transformed sentence into GOOD English. Check the vocabulary at the end of the book if you need help with the meanings of words.

1. Quintus gladium splendidum tenet.

   _____

   _____

2. Puella pūpam parvam numquam portat.

   _____

   _____

3. Servus magistrum iūcundum semper salūtat.

   _____

   _____

4. Drūsīlla et Matella paedagōgum īrātum clāmant.

   _____

   _____

5. Iūlius captīvum barbarum terret.

   _____

   _____

6. Rufus librum parvum nunc habet.

   _____

   _____

7. Aemilia histōriam splendidam auscultat.

   _____

   _____

8. Videtne Marcia sciūrum timidum in trīclīniō?

_____

_____

9. Taurus magnus rānam parvam videt.

_____

_____

10. Puella et puer fēminam Graecam respondet.

_____

_____

B) In the following exercise, circle the subject and draw a box around the direct object. Underline all adjectives that describe *the subject* once and all adjectives that describe *the direct object* twice. Then make the *whole* sentence plural—both subject and direct object. Remember: when the subject is plural, the verb must be plural, also! Finally, translate the transformed sentence into GOOD English. Use the vocabulary at the back of the book if you need help with the meaning of any words.

> **EXAMPLE:** Servus laetus taurum īrātum videt.
> Servī laetī taurōs īrātōs vident.
> The happy servants see the angry bulls.

1. Puella tunicam meam prōvidet.

_____

_____

2. Puer sciūrum timidum et parvum vocat.

_____

_____

3. Magister īrātus discipulum imparātum (unprepared) monet.

_____

_____

4. Servus parātus sellam movet.

_____

_____

5. Magister casam parvam nōn habitat.

_____

_____

6. Puella urnam magnam saepe portat.

_____

_____

7. Taurus ūmidus fīlium meum spectat.

_____

_____

8. Servus ad insulam parvam nāvigat.

_____

_____

Puellās videō.

NOMINATIVE OR ACCUSATIVE? SINGULAR OR PLURAL?

C) One word is missing in each of the following Latin sentences.

a) Look at the English translation and circle the word that is missing.

b) Determine whether your circled word is part of the *subject*, the *direct object*, or the *verb* of the sentence and write S, DO, or V in the blank on the left.

c) Finally, complete the sentence with the correct form of the missing Latin word. Be sure to use the correct ending!

1. _____ Quintus librum _____ tenet.
   Quintus is holding the big book.

2. _____ Servus _____ videt.
   The slave sees the donkey.

3. _____ Habetne cathēdram _____?
   Does he have a new chair?

4. _____ _____ Rōmānī sunt.
   The boys are Romans.

5. _____ Claudius _____ portat.
   Claudius carries the squirrels.

6. _____ _____ īrātae sunt.
   The servants are angry.

7. _____ Equōs _____ vocant.
   The farmers call the horses.

8. _____ Puellae asinum _____.
   The girls see the donkey.

Librōs habeō.

_____ **V. ANALYSIS EXERCISE** _____

> ### ANALYSIS QUESTION
>
> **What are linking verbs and transitive verbs?**

A) Look at the two sentences below and translate them into English on the lines provided.

1. Lāvīnia puella est.

   _____

2. Lāvīnia puellam videt.

   _____

NŌMEN _____

DIĒS _____

B) Now answer these questions based on the two Latin sentences by filling in the blanks or circling the appropriate response.

1. In sentence 1, *Lāvīnia* and *puella* are

   a) different people   **b)** the same person

2. In sentence 2, both *Lāvīnia* and *puella* are in the

   a) nominative case   **b)** accusative case

3. The verb in sentence 1 is _____.
   (WRITE THE VERB HERE)

4. Would it be fair to state the relationship between the word *Lāvīnia* and the word *puella* like this?

   Lāvīnia = puella   answer: _____

5. Now that you have studied the plural endings, finish this sentence correctly using sentence 1 as a model.

   Lāvīnia et Claudia _____ _____ .
   (VERB)   (NOUN)

   Could we replace the verb in this sentence with an equal sign?

   a) yes   **b)** no

CONCLUSION

The verb forms *est* and *sunt* are known as **linking verbs** because they link together two nouns that refer to the *same* person or thing.

Linking verbs are never followed by a direct object. Therefore, both nouns in

a sentence with *est* or *sunt* will always be in the _____ case.

When the verb of a sentence can be replaced by an equal sign (=) and the meaning of the sentence doesn't change substantially, you know you're dealing with a **linking verb**.

---

6. In sentence 2, *Lāvīnia* and *puella* refer to

    a) different people   **b)** the same person

7. In sentence 2, *Lāvīnia* is in the

    a) nominative case   **b)** accusative case

This indicates that *Lāvīnia* is the _____ of the sentence.

    a) subject   **b)** direct object.

8. In sentence 2, *puella* is in the

    a) nominative case   **b)** accusative case

This indicates that *puella* is the _____ of the sentence.

    a) subject   **b)** direct object

9. Can we replace the verb *videt* with an equal sign in sentence *2*?

    a) yes   **b)** no

10. Re-read the definition of a *linking verb* in the previous conclusion box, then complete the following statement.

The verb *vidēre* used in sentence 2 _____ a linking verb.
                                        (IS/IS NOT)

CONCLUSION

The verb *vidēre* (to see) is a **transitive verb**. A **transitive verb** shows that the action of seeing is *in transit* (i.e., moving) from *Lāvīnia* (the subject) to *puella* (the direct object).

Transitive verbs are regularly followed by a direct object.

In a sentence with a **transitive verb**, the subject noun is in the nominative case and the object noun is in the _____ case.

_____ VI. EXERCITĀTIŌNĒS _____

A) Circle the verb in each sentence below and underline the direct object (if there is one). Then, indicate if the verb is a *linking verb* (L) or a *transitive verb* (T).

_____ **1.** Atticus barbarus est captīvus.

_____ **2.** Atticus gladium in harēnā videt.

_____ **3.** Ōceanus magnus et lātus est.

_____ **4.** Caecilia discipulam studiōsam laudat.

_____ **5.** Portia et Gāia in vīllā hodiē sunt.

_____ **6.** Caecilia magistrōs suōs et patrem suum auscultat.

_____ **7.** Quintia est fēmina Hispāna.

_____ **8.** Fīlia sua est discipula occupāta.

_____ **9.** Trebius et Decius sciūrum parvum terrent.

_____ **10.** Histōriās narrat.

B) Now go back to Part A and translate the sentences.

1. _____

2. _____

3. _____

4. _____

5. _____

6. _____

7. _____

8. _____

9. _____

10. _____

FĀBULA

Trēs Puerī et Trēs Puellae in Circō Maximō

Marcia, Aemilia, et Portia puellae Rōmānae sunt. In Crētā habitant sed hodiē in Crētā nōn sunt. Nunc in Ītaliā sunt. Avunculum in Ītaliā vīsitant. Puellae sunt consōbrīnae.

Ecce, Decius et Rēgulus! Puerī sunt patruēlēs. Validī et clārī etiam sunt. In Crētā nōn habitant sed in Ītaliā. Puerī Rōmānī hodiē avunculum etiam vīsitant.

Quis est Theodorus? Estne Theodorus etiam puer Rōmānus? Minimē, nōn est. Puer Graecus est sed in Ītaliā habitat. Multī Graecī in Ītaliā habitant. Decius, Rēgulus, et Theodorus amīcī bonī et fīdī sunt.

Hodiē est diēs festus. Trēs puerī et trēs puellae sunt cum avunculō in Circō Maximō. Puerī et puellae multōs aurīgās et multōs equōs vident. Ecce, Octāvius! Aurīga fāmōsus est. Populus applaudat et puerī et puellae clāmant: "Optimus! Optimus est Octāvius, aurīga fāmōsus!"

Diēs festus est bonus. Puerī, puellae, et avunculus sunt contentī. Octāvius etiam contentus est. Victōria sua magna est!

INDEX VERBŌRUM

aurīga   (m. and f.) charioteer
avunculus*   uncle
Circus Maximus   a famous race track in Rome, see p. CLX.
consōbrīnus   (male) cousin on the mother's side

consōbrīna   (female) cousin on the mother's side
cum   (+ ablative) together with
diēs festus   holiday, festival day
multus, multa   many, much
patruēlis (patruēlēs)   (male or female) cousin on the father's side

* The Romans distinguished between *avunculus* (the mother's brother) and *patruus* (the father's brother). Both words translate into English as "uncle."

NŌMEN _____

DIĒS _____

VII. EXERCITĀTIŌNĒS

Read the English sentences below. Translate **only** the words in italics, making sure to put your translation into the proper case, gender, and number.

1. I especially like to eat different foreign *foods*.   _____

2. The family *papers* are kept in the safe.   _____

3. We haven't had time to wash the *big windows* yet.   _____

4. I like *my friends* because they are nice people.   _____

5. *Our books* are piled on the table.   _____

6. The animals *work* very hard and need a rest.   _____

7. My *name* is Quintus Caecilius Fēlix.   _____

8. The Appian Way is a *long* road built by the Romans.   _____

9. I saw the Tiber *river* when I was in Italy last year.   _____

10. *We don't see* many old cars on the roads these days.   _____

11. The girls are *tired and wet* and want to go to sleep.   _____

12. I asked the *tired girls* if they wanted to lie down for a while.   _____

13. *Five donkeys* were killed in the traffic accident.   _____

14. I prefer the *paper* in this book to the paper in that one.   _____

15. Roman *boys and girls* had to pay to go to school.   _____

LECTIO XVI

The Irregular Verb "TO BE"

"AURIGA FAMOSUS SUM"

I. ANALYSIS EXERCISE

ANALYSIS QUESTION

In what ways is the Latin verb *to be* irregular?

NŌMEN _____

DIĒS _____

In Chapters XI, XII, and XIII, we studied Latin verbs of the first conjugation (stem ending in *a*) and verbs of the second conjugation (stem ending in *e*). Because the verbs of the first and second conjugations follow a regular pattern, we call them *regular* verbs.

Once we know how to conjugate one verb of the first or second conjugation, we can conjugate all of the others simply by following the same patterns. For example, look at the two *new* verbs below and write out the full conjugation of each based on the pattern of the verbs conjugated on pages CLVIII and CLXXI.

APPELLŌ, APPELLĀRE, APPELLĀTUS
(to call, to name)

DOCEŌ, DOCĒRE, DOCTUS
(to teach)

_____	_____		_____	_____
_____	_____		_____	_____
_____	_____		_____	_____

In this chapter we are going to take a look at a verb that is *not* regular. Of course, it has a conjugation like all other verbs, but it does *not* follow a regular pattern. In fact, no other verb in the Latin language conjugates exactly like the verb *sum, esse*. Even its principal parts do not follow a regular pattern. For this reason, we call *sum, esse* an *irregular verb* (. . . makes sense, doesn't it?).

You are already familiar with two forms of this verb because we've been using them throughout this book: *est* and *sunt*. Now take a look at the complete conjugation of *sum, esse* (the verb *to be*) and compare it to the model regular verbs on pages CLVIII and CLXXI. When you have done that, answer the questions that follow.

THE IRREGULAR CONJUGATION OF THE VERB TO BE

sum, esse, futūrus (to be)

		SINGULAR		PLURAL
First person:	sum	I am	sumus	we are
Second person:	es	you (sing.) are	estis	you (plur.) are
Third person:	est	(he, she, it) is	sunt	they are

---

1. Look at the *personal endings* of the conjugation *sum, esse*. All of the *endings* are regular except for the _____ person _____. Write the form
_(SINGULAR/PLURAL) of the verb with the irregular ending in this space: _____

2. We find the stems of *regular* verbs by dropping the **-re** ending from the infinitive form. What is the infinitive form of the verb *to be*? _____. Does it contain the letters **-re** like all of the other verbs that we have studied? _____.

3. If we drop the personal endings from the six conjugated forms of the verb, are we left with only *one* stem or is there more than one stem? _____

4. Comparing this new verb with all of the others that you have studied, can you explain in your own words why we call it an irregular verb? _____

   _____

5. Go back to the Analysis Exercise on pages CCXLVIII–CCL. Reread the conclusions, then fill in the blanks below to complete the statement correctly.

CONCLUSION

Up to this point we have studied the two Latin verbs *est* and *sunt*. Both of these forms are known as _____ verbs. A _____ verb is *never* followed by a _____ because the function of a _____ verb is to *link* two nouns which are similar.

Because we have learned the full conjugation of this verb in this chapter, we can say that *all* forms of the verb *sum, esse* act as *linking verbs*. Because there will be no direct object in a sentence that contains any form of the verb *sum, esse*, both linked nouns will be in the _____ case.

_____ II. EXERCITĀTIŌNĒS _____

A) Fill in the proper form of the verb needed to complete the sentences.

1. (I am) Sextus _____.

2. (We are) Fīliae bonae _____.

3. (You are) Drūsīlla _____.

4. (You are) Drūsīlla et Matella _____.

5. (They are) Servī Hispānī _____.

6. (He is) Marcus Aurelius _____.

7. (She is) Discipula studiōsa _____.

8. (Is she) Ubi _____?

9. (You are) Aurīgae magnī _____.

10. (It is) Liber _____.

11. (Are we) _____ consōbrīnī?

12. (I am) Grammaticus Rōmānus _____.

13. (They are not) Contentī _____.

14. (You are) Discipulus bonus _____.

B) Write out the full Latin conjugation of the sentence below following the English model. Remember to change the noun to plural when necessary.

ENGLISH   LATIN

1. I am a good student.   _____

2. You (*singular*) are a good student.   _____

3. He/She is a good student.   _____

4. We are good students.   _____

5. You (*plural*) are good students.   _____

6. They are good students.   _____

C) Translate the following sentences into Latin. Be careful! Some sentences contain the linking verb and others contain transitive verbs. Be careful of the case of the nouns!

1. I am a good girl.

    _____

2. They are Roman boys.

    _____

3. I see the Roman boys.

    _____

4. The prisoners wound the angry bull.

    _____

5. They are angry.

    _____

6. Here is Theodorus! He is my son.

    _____

7. No, you are not Quintus and Tiberius.

    _____

8. Who am I?

_____

9. Are you Marcia?

_____

10. I think, therefore (ergō) I am.

_____

THE LAST WORD ON DERIVATIVES

Here is a list of 10 new Latin verbs. There are verbs from all four conjugations on the list. You do not have to memorize this list of words. They will not appear in any of the exercises in the rest of the book. Use the list, however, to help you see the Latin connection between some English words and their original Latin ancestors. Do the exercises below.

appellō, appellāre, appellātus to call, name

conveniō, convenīre, conventus to come together, assemble

dēleō, dēlēre, dēlētus to destroy

dēligō, dēligere, delectus to choose

doceō, docēre, doctus to teach

errō, errāre, errātus to wander

expellō, expellere, expulsus to drive out

pūniō, pūnīre, pūnītus to punish

stō, stāre, status to stand

trādō, trādere, trāditus to hand over, surrender

D) Each sentence in this exercise contains a word with which you may or may not be familiar. All of them are common English words. Using the list above, decide from which Latin verb each of the *italicized* words is derived, then complete the blanks with the *first two principal parts* of the appropriate verb and its English meaning.

1. The *docent* at the museum is a special guide who ____teaches us____ something about the collections housed in the museum.

    ___doceō, docēre___ = ____to teach____

2. When we make an error, we _____ from the truth.

    _____ = _____

3. When we *delete* a portion of a paragraph, what we are doing in reality is _____ part of it.

    _____ = _____

4. When we go to a *convention*, we go to a place where many people _____ .

    _____ = _____

5. A bank *statement* tells us what our financial _____ is.

    _____ = _____

6. Students who are *expelled* from school are _____ of the school by the authorities.

    _____ = _____

7. Criminals are *punished* for their crimes.

    _____ = _____

8. When we *trade* our salami sandwich for a friend's peanut butter and jelly sandwich, what we are really doing is _____ our sandwich for another one.

    _____ = _____

9. When teachers say that they insist on the proper scientific *appellation* on an exam, that teacher means he or she wants the proper scientific _____.

_____ = _____

10. When we *delegate* authority, we _____ someone else to carry out our wishes.

_____ = _____

E) Try these sentences on for size. See if you can fill in the blank and explain how these common English words came to mean what they mean.

1. A *fraternity* is a society of _____.

_____ = _____

2. A *sorority* is a society of _____.

_____ = _____

3. The *feminist* movement is a movement that asserts the rights of _____.

_____ = _____

4. Some men feel that their *virility* is endangered by the feminist movement. This means they feel that their _____-liness is at stake.

_____ = _____

5. The *maternity* ward in a hospital is the ward for_____.

_____ = _____

6. If I said that he gave her a *paternal* hug, you would know that
  a) he embraced her with mad, passionate love.
  b) hugged her as a father would hug his daughter.

_____ = _____

7. If I told you that Alice did it because she felt that it was her *filial* duty, you would know that she felt that it was her duty as a _____.

_____ = _____

8. If he regarded the child with *avuncular* pride, we know that he is probably her

_____ .

_____ = _____

F) Latin influenced not only the English language, but all of the Romance languages as well. Just for the fun of it, try to do the exercise below. Can you figure out the meaning of these **French** sentences using your knowledge of Latin? Check the verb list on pages CCLIX and the vocabulary at the end of the book for the meanings of the words in italics and use your common sense for the rest of the sentence. You might have to make some intelligent guesses to put the whole sentence together.

1. Le professeur *s'appelle* Marc Bertrand.

_____

The French word *s'appelle* probably comes from the Latin verb

_____ which means _____ .

2. La police *punit* le criminel.

_____

The French word *punit* probably comes from the Latin verb

_____ which means _____ .

3. Jacques *erre* sur les boulevards.

_____

The French word *erre* probably comes from the Latin verb

_____ which means _____ .

4. Marie *habite* dans un grand appartement.

_____

The French word *habite* probably comes from the Latin verb

_____ which means _____ .

5. Les spectateurs *répondent*: "Hourra!"

_____

The French word *répondent* probably comes from the Latin verb

_____ which means _____ .

G) Use your "Latin intuition" and your common sense to guess at the meanings of the following sentences in Spanish, Italian, and Romanian and translate them into GOOD English. Although the spelling of some of the words is slightly different, all of the key words are derived from Latin ancestors.

ITALIAN

1. Silvana porta cinque libri.

   ————————————————————————————————

2. La madre gusta la cena.

   ————————————————————————————————

3. La studentessa risponde alla questione.

   ————————————————————————————————

4. Carlo vede la casa nuova.

   ————————————————————————————————

NOMBRE _____

FECHA _____

El Toro

SPANISH

de = of   mi = my

1. La rana está en el agua.

   _____

2. La silla de mi amigo no es elegante.

   _____

3. El libro es antiguo.

   _____

4. La luna está clara.

   _____

ROMANIAN

1. Un program ideal de televiziune este informativ, educativ, interesant, şi amuzant.

   _____

2. Mariana ascultă muzică clasică.

   _____

3. Iulius intră în parcul frumos.

   _____

4. Gheorghe studează la universitatea în Bucureşti.

   _____

DUAE FĀBULAE

Consult the vocabulary lists at the end of the book for any words that you may not understand. The words in bold are explained in the short *Index Verbōrum* at the end of the stories.

Publius et Vīta Bona

Publius sum. Puer Rōmānus sum et in Etrūriā habitō. Sumus **sex** in familiā meā. Paterfamiliās est Fābricius Persius Prōcērus. Pater meus est negōtiātor fāmōsus. Clārus, bonus, et iustus est.

Quis est Antōnia? Māterfamiliās est. Fēmina formōsa et laeta est. Māter et pater hodiē in vīllā sunt.

Frātrem nōn habeō sed trēs sorōrēs habeō: Drūsīllam, Matellam, et Verginiam. Verginia puella parva est et pūpam antīquam habet. Multōs servōs in familiā habēmus. Grumio est paedagōgus et Cornēlius capsārius meus est. Tiberius in culīnā semper labōrat. Coquus optimus est. Familia mea est magna et in vīllā magnā habitāmus. **Vīta** bona est.

Trānio et Vīta Bona

Trānio sum. Puer Graecus sum sed in Ītaliā **cum** familiā habitō. In familiā meā sumus quinque. Paterfamiliās est Tēlemachus. Magister in scholā Rōmānā est. Pater est **lībertus.** Magister clārus et bonus est sed fāmōsus aut **pecūniōsus** nōn est.

Māterfamiliās est Aurelia et Rēgulus et Tullius frātrēs meī sunt. In **insulā** magnā habitāmus. Rōma multās insulās habet. Servōs nōn habēmus sed cibum bonum habēmus. Familia bona est. Vīta bona est.

INDEX VERBŌRUM

cum (+ ablative) together with
insula apartment house
lībertus freedman
negōtiātor (m.) businessman
   (especially a banker)

pecūniōsus, pecūniōsa rich,
   wealthy
sex six
vīta life

NOTĀ BENE

Notice the accusative case of the word *frāter* (*frātrem*). In this book, we have only studied first and second declension nouns. *Frāter* is a third declension noun and forms the accusative case in a different way from first and second declension nouns.

   What do you suppose is the accusative form of these words?

NOMINATIVE		ACCUSATIVE
frāter	=	*frātrem*
māter	=	_____
pater	=	_____

The accusative of *soror* (sister) is *sorōrem.*
The plural forms are *frātrēs, mātrēs, patrēs, sorōrēs.*

H) You have read the *Fābulae* about Publius and Trānio and their families. Now you are going to write a *Fābula* about your own family. Follow the directions carefully.

1. Study the *Index Verbōrum* below for the new vocabulary that you will need.

2. Read the English version of the *Fābula* as you fill in the blanks (in English) with the information requested.

3. Now, you are ready to translate your personal *Fābula* into Latin.
   a) Use your name and the names of the people in your family.
   b) Spell out the Roman numbers where needed. See page XXIII.
   c) Translate only what is appropriate for your family and eliminate the rest.

INDEX VERBŌRUM

aunt   amita (father's sister)
           mātertera (mother's sister)
brother   frāter (*plural* = frātrēs)
cousin   consōbrīna (*f.*) (on mother's side)
           consōbrīnus (*m.*) (on mother's side)
           patruēlis (*m. & f.*) (on father's side)

grandfather   avus
grandmother   avia
sister   soror (*plural* = sorōres)
uncle   avunculus (mother's brother)
           patruus (father's brother)

FĀBULA MEA

I am _____ . I am not a Roman boy/girl and I do not
            (YOUR NAME)

live in Italy. My family lives in America. There are (Sumus) _____
                                                              (NUMBER OF PEOPLE)

in my family; my father, _____ , my
                                       (NAME)

mother, _____ ; _____ brother(s),
                    (NAME)   (NUMBER)

_____ ;
                    (NAMES)

_____ sister(s), _____
(NUMBER)   (NAMES)

_____ ; my grandfather(s), _____
            (NAMES)

_____ ; my grandmother(s), _____
            (NAMES)

_____ ; _____ aunt(s),
                    (NAMES)   (NUMBER)

_____ uncle(s), _____ male cousins on my mother's side, _____ female cous-
(NUMBER)   (NUMBER)   (NUMBER)

ins on my mother's side and _____ male cousins on my father's side, and _____
                          (NUMBER)   (NUMBER)
female cousins on my father's side.

     My family _____ big. We _____ live in one house.
                        (IS/IS NOT)   (DO/DO NOT)
    In school, I am always a good student. My friends are good students, too. I like my friends and my school. Do you like your school?

FĀBULA MEA

_____

_____

_____

_____

_____

_____

_____

_____

_____

_____

_____

_____

_____

_____

_____

_____

_____

_____

APPENDIX

I. MODEL FIRST CONJUGATION VERB
(-ĀRE ENDING)

PORTŌ, PORTĀRE, PORTĀTUS (TO CARRY)

	LATIN		ENGLISH	
	singular	plural	singular	plural
1st pers.	portō	portāmus	I carry	we carry
2nd pers.	portās	portātis	you (sing.) carry	you (plur.) carry
3rd pers.	portat	portant	he, she, it carries	they carry

II. MODEL SECOND CONJUGATION VERB
(-ĒRE ENDING)

HABEŌ, HABĒRE, HABITUS (TO HAVE)

	LATIN		ENGLISH	
	singular	plural	singular	plural
1st pers.	habeō	habēmus	I have	we have
2nd pers.	habēs	habētis	you (sing.) have	you (plur.) have
3rd pers.	habet	habent	he, she, it has	they have

III. THE IRREGULAR VERB

SUM, ESSE, FUTŪRUS (TO BE)

	LATIN		ENGLISH	
	singular	plural	singular	plural
1st pers.	sum	sumus	I am	we are
2nd pers.	es	estis	you (sing.) are	you (plur.) are
3rd pers.	est	sunt	he, she, it is	they are

IV. PREFIXES

LATIN PREFIXES	ENGLISH MEANINGS
ab-, a-	from, away
ad-	to, toward, near
ante-	before
con-, col-	with, against, together
de-	away, down
ex-, e-	out of, out from
in-, im-	into, in, not
post-	after
pre-	before
re-	again, back
sub-, sup-	under, below
trans-	across, through

V. SUFFIXES

LATIN SUFFIXES	ENGLISH MEANINGS
-able, -ible	able to be
-al	pertaining to
-ary, -ory	relating to
-ate	do, make, cause
-ment	condition or quality
-or, -tor, -er	one who
-ous	full of
-tion, -sion	act or state of

VI. LATIN LOCUTIONS USED IN ENGLISH

LATIN	ENGLISH MEANING
ad nauseam	to the point of disgust or boredom
in absēntiā	in one's absence
notā bene	attention! please note!
per capita	apiece, for each individual
per sē	by itself
status quō	the existing state of affairs
tempus fugit	time flies
terra fīrma	solid ground
via	by way of
vice versā	the other way around

VII. INDEX VERBORUM—LATIN/ENGLISH

NOUNS

agricola (m.) farmer
amīca (female) friend
amīcus (male) friend
amita aunt (father's sister)
aqua water
arbor (f.); (acc.: arbōrem) tree
asinus donkey, ass
asparagus asparagus
aurīga (m. or f.) charioteer (male or female)
avia grandmother
avunculus uncle (mother's brother)
avus grandfather
calamus a reed pen
ṣārius a slave who carried his young master's satchel to school
captīvus prisoner
casa cottage, hut
cathēdra chair
cēna dinner, the principal meal of the Romans
charta paper
cibus food
Circus Maximus famous racetrack in Rome (see p. 160)
consōbrīna (female) cousin on the mother's side
consōbrīnus (male) cousin on the mother's side
coquus cook
crēta chalk
culīna kitchen
diēs (m.); (acc.: diem) day
diēs festus holiday, festival day
discipula (female) student
discipulus (male) student
equus horse
exercitātio (f.); (plur.: exercitātiōnēs) exercise
fābula tale, story
fāma fame, reputation
familia family
fēmina woman
fenestra window
fīlia daughter
fīlius son

fluvius stream, river
frāter (plur.: frātrēs) brother
fungus mushroom
Gallia France
gallīna hen
gallus rooster
gladiātor gladiator (one hired to fight at public shows)
gladius sword
glōria glory, fame
Graecia Greece
grammaticus a grammarian, secondary school teacher
harēna sand (by extension: the arena of the amphitheater)
historia history
hortus garden
ientāculum (n.) breakfast
imperium (n.) empire
index verbōrum vocabulary list
insula island, apartment house
lacus lake
lectio (f.); (plur.: lectiōnēs) a picking-out, a selecting (chapter)
lectus bed
liber book
lībertus freedman
litterātor teacher (especially of elementary school)
lūdus elementary school
lūna moon
magister teacher (elementary school)
māter (3rd decl.); (acc.: mātrem) mother
māterfamiliās mother of the family, female head of the family
mātertera aunt (mother's sister)
murus wall
narrātio (f.); (plur.: narrātiōnēs) a telling, a relating
narrātor (m.); (acc.: narrātōrem) narrator, storyteller
negōtiātor (m.); (acc.: negōtiātōrem) businessman (especially a banker)
nōmen name
ōceanus ocean

oliva   olive
paedagōgus   slave who accompanied children to and from school
papȳrus   paper
pater (3rd decl.); (acc.: patrem)   father
paterfamiliās   father of the family, male head of the family
patruēlis (m. and f.); (plur.: patruēlēs)   (male or female) cousin on the father's side
patruus   uncle (father's brother)
plūma   pen (a quill pen)
poēta   poet
populus   people
porcīna   pork
porta   door
prandium (n.)   lunch
puella   girl
puer (acc.: puerum)   boy
pūpa   doll
quaestio (f.); (plur.: quaestiōnēs)   a seeking, a searching (question)
rāna   frog

rhētor   a teacher of rhetoric, an orator
schola   secondary school
sciūrus   squirrel
sella   chair
senātor (m.); (senātōrem)   senator
serva   (female) slave or servant
servus   (male) slave or servant
soror (plur.: sorōrēs)   sister
stilus   a pointed bone instrument for writing on a waxed tablet
tabella   small flat board or tablet
tabula   notebook, writing tablet
taurus   bull
terra   earth, land
trīclīnium (n.)   dining couch, dining room
tunica   tunic (see p. 136)
urna   vase
via   road, way
victōria   victory
vīlla   country house, estate
vir (acc.: virum)   man
vīta   life

ADJECTIVES

albus, alba   white
antiquus, antiqua   old, ancient (applied to things but not to people)
barbarus, barbara   foreign, uncultivated, strange
bonus, bona   good
clārus, clāra   bright, famous, clear
contentus, contenta   satisfied
dīvīsus, dīvīsa   divided
fāmōsus, fāmōsa   famous
fatīgātus, fatīgāta   weary, tired
ferus, fera   wild, untamed
fīdus, fīda   faithful
formōsus, formōsa   beautiful, handsome
fuscus, fusca   dark, black
Graecus, Graeca   Greek
Hispānus, Hispāna   Spanish
honestus, honesta   honored, honorable, respectable
inimīcus, inimīca   unfriendly
īrātus, īrāta   angry

iūcundus, iūcunda   pleasant, agreeable, delightful
iustus, iusta   just, fair
laetus, laeta   happy
lātus, lāta   wide, broad
Latīnus, Latīna   Latin
longus, longa   long
magnus, magna   big
malus, mala   bad
maximus, maxima   biggest, very big
meus, mea   my
multus, multa   many, much
noster, nostra   our
novus, nova   new
occupātus, occupāta   busy, occupied
optimus, optima   very good, best
parātus, parāta   ready, prepared
parvus, parva   little, small
pecūniōsus, pecūniōsa   rich, wealthy
prōcērus, prōcēra   tall
pūblicus, pūblica   public

Rōmānus, Rōmāna   Roman
sex   six
splendidus, splendida   splendid, magnificent
studiōsus, studiōsa   eager, studious
stultus, stulta   silly, foolish
stupidus, stupida   stupid, dull

suus, sua   his or her (own)
timidus, timida   timid, fearful
tranquillus, tranquilla   calm, quiet
tuus, tua   your (sing.)
ūmidus, ūmida   wet, moist
validus, valida   strong, muscular
vester, vestra   your (plur.)

VERBS

THIRD PERSON SINGULAR—PRESENT

amat   (he, she, it) loves
ambulat   (he, she, it) walks
auscultat   (he, she, it) listens (to)
clāmat   (he, she, it) calls or shouts
est   (he, she, it) is (does not take a direct object)
habet   (he, she, it) has (takes a direct object)
habitat   (he, she, it) lives
lacrimat   (he, she, it) cries or weeps

locat   (he, she, it) puts, places
monet   (he, she, it) warns or advises
narrat   (he, she, it) relates, tells
portat   (he, she, it) carries
pugnat   (he, she, it) fights
pulsat   (he, she, it) hits or strikes
sunt   they are
tenet   (he, she, it) holds
terminat   (he, she, it) finishes or ends
videt   (he, she, it) sees

DICTIONARY FORM

ambulō, ambulāre, ambulātus   to walk
amō, amāre, amātus   to love
auscultō, auscultāre, auscultātus   to listen (to)
cēnō, cēnāre, cēnātus   to eat dinner, to dine
clāmō, clāmāre, clāmātus   to call, to shout
cōgitō, cōgitāre, cōgitātus   to think
gustō, gustāre, gustātus   to taste
habeō, habēre, habitus   to have
habitō, habitāre, habitātus   to live
intrō, intrāre, intrātus (followed by in + acc.)   to enter, to walk into
labōrō, labōrāre, labōrātus   to work, to toil
lacrimō, lacrimāre, lacrimātus   to cry, to weep
laudō, laudāre, laudātus   to praise
locō, locāre, locātus   to place, to put
moneō, monēre, monitus   to warn, to advise
moveō, movēre, mōtus   to move
narrō, narrāre, narrātus   to relate, to tell
nāvigō, nāvigāre, nāvigātus   to sail

parō, parāre, parātus   to prepare, to ready
portō, portāre, portātus   to carry
prōvideō, prōvidēre, provīsus   to provide, to foresee
pugnō, pugnāre, pugnātus   to fight
pulsō, pulsāre, pulsātus   to strike, to hit
respondeō, respondēre, respōnsus   to reply, to answer
rīdeō, rīdēre, rīsus   to laugh, to smile
salūtō, salūtāre, salūtātus   to greet
sedeō, sedēre, sessus   to sit
spectō, spectāre, spectātus   to watch, to look at
sum, esse, futūrus (irreg.)   to be
teneō, tenēre, tentus   to hold
terminō, termināre, terminātus   to finish, to end
terreō, terrēre, territus   to frighten
videō, vidēre, vīsus   to see
vīsitō, vīsitāre, vīsitātus   to visit
vocō, vocāre, vocātus   to call, to invite
vulnerō, vulnerāre, vulnerātus   to wound

────────────────── OTHER ──────────────────

ad (+ accusative) to, towards
aut or
cum (+ ablative) together with
Ecce . . . ! Here is! There is (over there)! Behold!
ergō therefore
et and
etiam also, likewise, still
hodiē today
in (+ ablative) in, on
in (+ accusative) into
ita (+ a verb) certainly, (yes)
ita vērō (+ a verb) certainly! (yes!)
iterum again
minimē (+ a verb) not at all, no

nōn not (usually precedes the verb)
numquam never
nunc now
prope (+ accusative) next to, near (to)
quid? what?
quis? who?
quoque also
saepe mostly, generally
salvē greetings
sed but
semper always
ubi? where?
valē good-bye
vērō truly

──────── VIII. INDEX VERBŌRUM—ENGLISH/LATIN ────────

────────────────── NOUNS ──────────────────

apartment house insula
arena harēna
asparagus asparagus
ass asinus
aunt (father's sister) amita
aunt (mother's sister) mātertera
banker negōtiātor (m.); (acc.: negōtiātōrem)
bed lectus
book liber
boy puer (acc.: puerum)
breakfast ientāculum (n.)
brother frāter (plur.: frātrēs)
bull taurus
businessman negōtiātor (m.); (acc.: negōtiātōrem)
chair cathēdra, sella
chalk crēta
chapter lectio (f.); (acc.: lectiōnem)
charioteer aurīga (m. and f.)
cook coquus
cottage casa

cousin (female on mother's side) consōbrīna
cousin (male on mother's side) consōbrīnus
cousin (male or female on father's side) patruēlis (m. and f.); (plur.: patruēlēs)
daughter fīlia
day diēs (m.); (acc.: diem)
dining couch trīclīnium (n.)
dining room trīclīnium (n.)
dinner cēna
doll pūpa
donkey asinus
door porta
earth terra
empire imperium (n.)
exercise exercitātio (plur.: exercitātiōnēs)
fame fāma, glōria
family familia
farmer agricola (m.)

father pater (3rd declension), paterfamiliās
festival day diēs festus
food cibus
France Gallia
freedman lībertus
friend (female) amīca
friend (male) amīcus
frog rāna
garden hortus
girl puella
gladiator gladiātor (acc.: gladiātōrem)
glory glōria
grandfather avus
grandmother avia
Greece Graecia
hen gallīna
history historia
holiday diēs festus
horse equus
house (cottage, hut) casa
house (country house, estate) vīlla
hut casa
island insula
kitchen culīna
lake lacus
land terra
life vīta
lunch prandium (n.)
man vir (m.); (acc.: virum)
moon lūna
mother māter (3rd declension), māter-familiās
mushroom fungus
name nōmen
narrator narrātor (m.); (acc.: narrātōrem)
notebook tabula, tabella
ocean ōceanus
olive oliva
orator rhētor
paper charta, papȳrus
pen (a reed pen) calamus
pen (bone instrument for writing on wax tablets) stilus
pen (quill pen) plūma
people populus
poet poēta (m.)
pork porcīna

prisoner captīvus
question quaestio (f.); (acc.: quaestiōnem)
racetrack example: Circus Maximus
reputation fāma
river fluvius
road via
rooster gallus
sand harēna
school (elementary) lūdus
school (secondary school) schola
servant (female) serva
servant (male) servus
sister soror (f.); (plur.: sorōres)
slave who carried master's books to school capsārius
slave (female) serva
slave (male) servus
slave who accompanied children to school paedagōgus
son fīlius
squirrel sciūrus
story fābula, narrātio (f.)
storyteller narrātor (m.); (acc.: narrātōrem)
stream fluvius
student (female) discipula
student (male) discipulus
sword gladius
tablet (for writing) tabula, tabella
tale fābula, narrātio (f.); (acc.: narrātiōnem)
teacher (elementary school) magister, litterātor
teacher (of rhetoric) rhētor
teacher (secondary school) grammaticus
tree arbor (f.); (acc.: arbōrem)
tunic tunica (see p. 136)
uncle (father's brother) patruus
uncle (mother's brother) avunculus
vase urna
victory victōria
vocabulary index verbōrum
wall murus
water aqua
way (roadway) via
window fenestra
woman fēmina

agreeable   iūcundus, iūcunda
ancient   antiquus, antiqua (used for things, not persons)
angry   īrātus, īrāta
bad   malus, mala
beautiful   formōsus, formōsa
best   optimus, optima
big   magnus, magna
big (very big)   maximus, maxima
biggest   maximus, maxima
black   fuscus, fusca
bright   clārus, clāra
broad   lātus, lāta
busy   occupātus, occupāta
calm   tranquillus, tranquilla
clear   clārus, clāra
dark   fuscus, fusca
delightful   iūcundus, iūcunda
divided   dīvīsus, dīvīsa
dull   stupidus, stupida
eager   studiōsus, studiōsa
fair   iustus, iusta
faithful   fīdus, fīda
famous   clārus, clāra/fāmōsus, fāmōsa
fearful   timidus, timida
foolish   stultus, stulta
foreign   barbarus, barbara
good   bonus, bona
good (very good)   optimus, optima
Greek   Graecus, Graeca
handsome   formōsus, formōsa
happy   laetus, laeta
her (own)   suus, sua
his (own)   suus, sua
honorable   honestus, honesta
honored   honestus, honesta
just   iustus, iusta
Latin   Latīnus, Latīna
little   parvus, parva
long   longus, longa

magnificent   splendidus, splendida
many   multi, multae
moist   ūmidus, ūmida
much   multus, multa
my   meus, mea
occupied   occupātus, occupāta
old   antiquus, antiqua (used for things, not persons)
our   noster, nostra
pleasant   iūcundus, iūcunda
prepared   parātus, parāta
public   pūblicus, pūblica
quiet   tranquillus, tranquilla
ready   parātus, parāta
respectable   honestus, honesta
rich   pecūniōsus, pecūniōsa
Roman   Rōmānus, Rōmāna
satisfied   contentus, contenta
silly   stultus, stulta
six   sex
small   parvus, parva
Spanish   Hispānus, Hispāna
splendid   splendidus, splendida
strange   barbarus, barbara
studious   studiōsus, studiōsa
stupid   stupidus, stupida
tall   prōcērus, prōcēra
timid   timidus, timida
tired   fatīgātus, fatīgāta
uncultivated   barbarus, barbara
unfriendly   inimīcus, inimīca
untamed   ferus, fera
wealthy   pecūniōsus, pecūniōsa
weary   fatīgātus, fatīgāta
wet   ūmidus, ūmida
white   albus, alba
wide   lātus, lāta
wild   ferus, fera
your (plur.)   vester, vestra
your (sing.)   tuus, tua

(he, she, it) advises   monet
(they) are   sunt
(he, she, it) calls (shouts)   clāmat
(he, she, it) carries   portat
(he, she, it) cries (weeps)   lacrimat
(he, she, it) ends   terminat
(he, she, it) fights   pugnat
(he, she, it) finishes   terminat
(he, she, it) has   habet (takes a
   direct object)
(he, she, it) hits   pulsat
(he, she, it) holds   tenet

(he, she, it) is   est (does not take a
   direct object)
(he, she, it) listens (to)   auscultat
(he, she, it) lives   habitat
(he, she, it) loves   amat
(he, she, it) places   locat
(he, she, it) puts   locat
(he, she, it) sees   videt
(he, she, it) shouts   clāmat
(he, she, it) strikes (hits)   pulsat
(he, she, it) walks   ambulat
(he, she, it) warns   monet

to advise   moneō, monēre, monītus
to answer   respondeō, respondēre,
   respōnsus
to be   sum, esse, futūrus (irreg.)
to call (invite)   vocō, vocāre, vocātus
to call (shout)   clāmō, clāmāre,
   clāmātus
to carry   portō, portāre, portātus
to cry (weep)   lacrimō, lacrimāre,
   lacrimātus
to dine   cēnō, cēnāre, cēnātus
to eat dinner   cēnō, cēnāre, cēnātus
to end   terminō, termināre,
   terminātus
to enter   intrō, intrāre, intrātus
   (followed by in + accus.)
to fight   pugnō, pugnāre, pugnātus
to finish   terminō, termināre,
   terminātus
to foresee   prōvideō, prōvidēre,
   prōvīsus
to frighten   terreō, terrēre, territus
to get ready   parō, parāre, parātus
to greet   salūtō, salūtāre, salūtātus
to have   habeō, habēre, habitus
to hit   pulsō, pulsāre, pulsātus
to hold   teneō, tenēre, tentus
to invite (call)   vocō, vocāre, vocātus
to laugh   rīdeō, rīdēre, rīsus
to listen (to)   auscultō, auscultāre,
   auscultātus
to live   habitō, habitāre, habitātus
to look at   spectō, spectāre, spectātus

to love   amō, amāre, amātus
to move   moveō, movēre, mōtus
to place   locō, locāre, locātus
to praise   laudō, laudāre, laudātus
to prepare   parō, parāre, parātus
to provide   prōvideō, prōvidēre,
   prōvīsus
to put   locō, locāre, locātus
to ready   parō, parāre, parātus
to relate (tell)   narrō, narrāre, narrātus
to reply   respondeō, respondēre,
   respōnsus
to sail   nāvigō, nāvigāre, nāvigātus
to see   videō, vidēre, vīsus
to shout   clāmō, clāmāre, clāmātus
to sit   sedeō, sedēre, sessus
to smile   rīdeō, rīdēre, rīsus
to strike (hit)   pulsō, pulsāre, pulsātus
to taste   gustō, gustāre, gustātus
to tell   narrō, narrāre, narrātus
to think   cōgitō, cōgitāre, cōgitātus
to toil   labōrō, labōrāre, labōrātus
to visit   vīsitō, vīsitāre, vīsitātus
to walk   ambulō, ambulāre, ambulātus
to walk into   intrō, intrāre, intrātus
   (followed by in + accus.)
to warn   moneō, monēre, monītus
to watch   spectō, spectāre, spectātus
to weep   lacrimō, lacrimāre,
   lacrimātus
to work   labōrō, labōrāre, labōrātus
to wound   vulnerō, vulnerāre,
   vulnerātus

again	iterum	**not**	nōn (usually precedes the verb)
also	etiam, quoque	**not at all (no)**	minimē (+ a verb)
always	semper	**now**	nunc
and	et	**or**	aut
Behold!	Ecce!	**still**	etiam

again   iterum
also   etiam, quoque
always   semper
and   et
Behold!   Ecce!
but   sed
certainly (yes)   ita (+ a verb)
certainly! (yes!)   ita vērō (+ a verb)
generally   saepe
good-bye   valē
greetings   salvē
hello   salvē
Here is . . . !   Ecce . . . !
in   in (+ ablative)
into   in (+ accusative)
likewise   etiam
mostly   saepe
near (to)   prope (+ accusative)
never   numquam
next to   prope (+ accusative)
no   (not directly translatable; use "not at all")

not   nōn (usually precedes the verb)
not at all (no)   minimē (+ a verb)
now   nunc
or   aut
still   etiam
There (over there) is . . . !   Ecce . . . !
therefore   ergō
to (towards)   ad (+ accusative)
today   hodiē
together with   cum (+ ablative)
too   quoque, etiam
towards   ad (+ accusative)
truly   vērō
what?   quid?
where?   ubi?
who?   quis?
yes   (not directly translatable; use "certainly")
yes!   (not directly translatable; use "certainly!")

VALE! BONAM FORTŪNAM!